Storytelling in Organizations

Storytelling in Organizations

Why Storytelling Is Transforming 21st Century
Organizations and Management

John Seely Brown
Stephen Denning
Katalina Groh
Laurence Prusak

Elsevier Butterworth–Heinemann
200 Wheeler Road, Burlington, MA 01803, USA
Linacre House, Jordan Hill, Oxford OX2 8DP, UK

∞   Recognizing the importance of preserving what has been written, Elsevier prints
    its books on acid-free paper whenever possible.

Library of Congress Cataloging-in-Publication Data

Storytelling in organizations: why storytelling is transforming 21st century organizations
    and management/John Seely Brown ... [et al].
        p. cm.
    Includes index.
    ISBN 0-7506-7820-8 (alk. paper)
        1. Communication in management. 2. Communication in organizations.
    3. Storytelling. 4. Corporate culture. I. Brown, John Seely.

    HD30.3.S765 2004
    658.4'5--dc22   2004051873

British Library Cataloguing-in-Publication Data
A catalogue record for this book is available from the British Library.

ISBN: 0-7506-7820-8

For information on all Butterworth–Heinemann publications
visit our Web site at www.bh.com

04 05 06 07 08 09 10   10 9 8 7 6 5 4 3 2 1

Printed in the United States of America

Table of Contents

Preface: Stephen Denning

This book tells how four busy executives, each coming from a different background, each with a very different perspective, were surprised to find themselves converge on the idea of narrative as an extraordinarily valuable lens for understanding and managing organizations in the 21st century. It reflects a conversation that took place under the auspices of The Smithsonian Associates in April 2001 and the effects that this conversation has stimulated since then.

The authors are four very different people:

- Larry Prusak has a background as a historian and worked as an executive and researcher in a giant computer firm—IBM.
- John Seely Brown is a scientist with a background in mathematics and computer sciences and was the Chief Scientist of the Xerox Corporation until 2002.
- Katalina Groh studied finance and economics and now creates and distributes educational films for her own firm—Groh Productions.
- I was trained as a lawyer and was director of knowledge management at the World Bank.

Although our journeys started from different sources, our four independent journeys ended up in the same place. None of us either by background or inclination expected to be involved in narrative and storytelling. But each of us noticed the surprising importance and pervasiveness of narrative and storytelling in our respective settings. Each of us was excited that our understanding of narrative could be used to practical advantage.

We all worked in environments where storytelling was widely seen as something frivolous and ephemeral, something relevant mainly to entertainment, or something that only children and primitive societies engage in. Yet each of us became convinced that narrative and storytelling played an enormous role in the modern economy and in organizations in the public and private sector—the serious aspects of 21st century life. In fact, we have come to see that narrative has a hand in practically everything that happens of any significance in human affairs. And each of us is convinced that storytelling will play a larger explicit role in the future than we would have expected only a few years ago.

This book then is the account of the trajectories that we have each followed to discover the importance of storytelling for management and organizations.

How the First Smithsonian Associates Event Started

Late in 2000, a friend introduced me to Mara Mayor, the director of The Smithsonian Associates, and I talked to her about the idea of launching a symposium on organizational storytelling in Washington DC. Her initial reaction was, "This is an unlikely topic. Do you think anyone would attend?"

I told her my story, and she said "Yes, that *is* interesting. Who else could you line up?" After Larry Prusak and John Seely Brown and Katalina Groh had agreed to participate, she agreed to do it. In fact, she actually came and opened the event with the imposing title of: "Storytelling: Passport to the 21st Century."

I guess we were all wondering how many people would show up for the event. But it turned out that so many people signed up for it, we had to hire a larger auditorium.

The Aftermath of the 2001 Symposium

The Smithsonian symposium of 2001 was an exciting event for those who participated in it, and it has continued to have significant ripple effects.

One immediate result of the symposium was the launching of a website that enabled the conversation that took place to reach tens of thousands of people beyond those who were physically present in April 2001.[1]

Another direct consequence has been the formation of groups of professionals interested in organizational storytelling. The first of these was in Washington DC. The group, which has come to call itself the Golden Fleece Group, has been meeting on a monthly basis since June 2001. In these meetings, the participants share what they have been doing, or try out new ideas. They also participated in an improv theater event related to another book on storytelling.[2] Other similar groups have emerged in other parts of the country.[3] The groups share views among each other from time to time on topics of common interest.

The Smithsonian symposium itself has also become an annual phenomenon. April in Washington has come to mean organizational storytelling at The Smithsonian Associates. In 2004, the event expanded so that there was a whole weekend of storytelling activities surrounding the symposium at the core. The event now has an international attendance with participants from countries such as Canada, the UK, Denmark, New Zealand, and Brazil.

The message of organizational storytelling is also starting to appear in the management literature. From 2002 onward, the importance of storytelling has been highlighted with articles in Booz Allen's *strategy+business*, the *Harvard Business Review* and the *Wall Street Journal*.[4]

Organizational storytelling is also beginning to appear as an academic topic in universities. For instance, Georgetown University in Washington, DC now has an undergraduate course in storytelling as part of their curriculum. Until recently narrative has typically been merely an item in a broader knowledge management course or management program; now, it's beginning to be treated as a subject in itself.

THE ROLE OF THIS BOOK

This book is a continuation of the conversation that was launched in 2001. In putting this text before you, we, the authors, believe that the discussion has enduring value. Each chapter includes the presentation that was made in 2001, as well as the reflections of the author, three years later in 2004. We hope that in this format the conversation can reach even more people and stimulate further new discussions and activities in organizational storytelling.

In promoting the cause of narrative, we're obviously not opposed to science. Nor are we proposing to abandon analysis. Where science and analysis can make progress and make a useful contribution, we should use them. Where they can't or don't, they should step aside and let narrative contribute. We're trying to bridge the distance between science and narrative and still retain the value of both. Our aspiration is a marriage of narrative and analysis.

This book doesn't purport to be a comprehensive treatment of organizational storytelling. The authors don't necessarily agree with each other in every detail. Readers will see that some of us are more optimistic about the possibilities for technology than others. Time will tell which leads prove to be the most productive. In presenting different perspectives on issues such as these, we hope to spark some new insights from the reader.

We are less interested in putting forward a theory of narrative than we are in putting before you some idea sparkers and in radiating possibility. We're exploring the thought that narrative has substantial practical value in organizations for dealing with many of the principal challenges facing managers and leaders today.

ENDNOTES

1 http://www.creatingthe21stcentury.org

2 Stephen Denning: *Squirrel Inc.: A Fable of Leadership Through Storytelling*. (Jossey-Bass, May 2004).

3 In San Diego, there is the *StoryWork Community of Practice* group and in Boston, there is *Storytelling in Organizations-Boston* (SIO-B).

4 (1) Bill Birchard: "Once upon a Time" in *strategy+business*, 2nd Quarter 2002. http://www.strategy-business.com/press/article/18637?pg=0 (March 8, 2004). (2) "Storytelling That Moves People: A Conversation with Screenwriter Coach, Robert McKee." *Harvard Business Review*, June 2003, page 51. (3) Stephen Denning, "Telling Tales" *Harvard Business Review*, May 2004. (4) Julie Bennett: "Spin Straw into Gold with Good Storytelling." *Wall Street Journal*, July 30, 2003. http://www.startupjournal.com/ideas/services/20030730-bennett.html (March 8, 2004). (5) Julie Bennett: "Storytelling & Diversity." *Wall Street Journal*, July 8, 2003. http://www.careerjournal.com/myc/diversity/20030708-bennett.html

ONE

How We Got into Storytelling

Economic institutions will look to some degree like religious cere-monies or social gatherings. They will need to be read in terms of human intentions and beliefs.

—Deirdre McCloskey[1]

LARRY PRUSAK: HOW I CAME TO STORYTELLING

To some people—people in business, people in management, people running public sector organizations—storytelling might seem like an odd subject to be talking about at all. The thought that narrative and storytelling might be important ideas in organizational thinking in the coming century might seem even odder. So, at the outset, let me say how I came to see the importance of narrative and story-telling. For me, there were three main roads.

How Are Norms Transmitted?

I started out in life as a history professor, college-level, on the history of ideas, the history of culture and, so forth. So I would teach and bore freshman students in World Civilization and subjects like that. This was European and Asian history. As it happened, I never studied American history.

But one day, I happened to read Alexis de Tocqueville's *Democracy in America*, one of the great books of the world. And I was astounded, because it read like a Baedeker for America in 1968, the year that I read it, rather than something written in the 1840s. It was absolutely accurate. If you have read it, you'll know what I'm talking about. It's a complete and accurate guide to America, but it's old. The people that de Tocqueville spoke to are no longer living, and yet we act the same way. This book is an extraordinarily good guide to what America is like.

> The people de Tocqueville spoke to are no longer living, but his book is still a good guide to what America is like. How could this be?

So I asked myself: "How could this be?" It never occurred to me to ask myself at the time: "What are the carriers of behavioral norms? What are the ways that we learn how to behave that continue through time? How does this happen?"

Historians don't really talk much about this. So I began asking questions of people. I said: "Do anthropologists know about this? Do cultural historians? Who knows about this?" And I couldn't get any good answers. I was at a university and I would hang around other universities, and no one could say what are the carriers of information about behavior that people pick up, and that last for 100 years or more. If you go to Ireland or England, you'll see that they may last 800 hundred years. With the Palestinians and the Israelis, maybe 3000 years.

People have remarkably stable behavior over time. Now it does change. But it doesn't change that much. The continuity and endurance of behavioral norms have a great deal to do with stories. I didn't learn this till years later. But that's what I think it is. Stories from the Bible. Stories of atrocities. Stories about our history. Not so long ago, a woman friend of mine was in Kosovo, where she interviewed grandparents who told stories to their children, their grandchildren, about atrocities that occurred in the 14th century. They raised these children from an early age with stories like: "Think about what this other group did your ancestors!" And these stories have tremendous salience. The way Bible stories do. The way all sorts of stories do. That's one road by which I came to storytelling.

How Do Organizations Work?

Another road that may be more pertinent to organizations and management is the failure of the standard model to account for how organizations really work in practice. What's taught in business schools, and what's taught in training and development classes and in most corporations, has very little to do with how organizations really work. It's worse than Plato's cave—there are not even shadows. It's a question of using an incorrect metaphor—the metaphor of the machine. Among the many ways this metaphor fails is its failure to explain how people learn how to act in organizations.

> *It's worse than Plato's cave. There are not even any shadows.*

- Where is the knowledge in organizations?
- How do you know what people know?
- How do you know how to behave?
- How do you know how to act when you enter an organization?

Many of the answers to questions can be understood through stories. That's another reason to study stories.

An aspect that interests me—I'm a kind of economist *manqué*—relates to how much of the economic activity in the United States and in all industrial countries has to do with talking and persuasion. A number of years ago, a well-known economist, Deirdre McCloskey, wrote an article in the *American Economic Review* showing that 28% of the gross national product (GNP) in the United States is accounted for by persuasion.[2] She did the math, and the numbers are remarkable, if you think about it. Law. Public relations. The ministry. Psychology. Marketing. What do these people do? They persuade other people. The fact is that we all do a lot of this. Some people have other words for it than persuasion, which I won't go into here. Be that as it may, when you try to persuade someone of something, a big piece of that is telling them stories. If persuasion is 28% of the GNP, you could make a good argument that around two-thirds of that is clever storytelling. On that basis, storytelling would have amounted in 1999 to activities valued at US $1.8 trillion, a number of decidedly non-trivial dimensions.[3]

What Do CEOs Actually Do?

The other road concerns the role of CEOs. We all read about the large salaries that CEOs get. Many of us find the disparity between what they earn and what other people earn as immoral and abhorrent. For many years, I never really saw a CEO do anything that was wildly different from what I could do or what most people could do in an organization. So I always used to wonder: why are they paid so much?

And then one day, I went to a meeting. It was a meeting on Wall Street where Lou Gerstner, the CEO of IBM, met the market analysts. And lo and behold, I was asked to come to this meeting. Gerstner is an irascible kind of guy, not that charming. I asked myself: "What does he do that other people don't do?" So we go into a room and there are people from the various banks and the brokers and the analysts and Gerstner starts telling them stories. Stories about IBM. Stories about the future of IBM. These were stories. He couldn't tell them facts about the future. He was telling them what IBM was going to do. It was all stories. And it worked. It really worked. And so I said to myself, "So that's what they do!"

> Jack Welch was asked his most important attribute and he said, "What really counts is that I'm Irish and I knows how to tell stories."

Now I could begin to understand what CEOs do: they tell stories. It must be worth a lot, because when there's a "Buy" rather than a "Sell" or a "Hold," that makes a lot of money for the stakeholders. I don't want to discus the moral basis of capitalism here, but I could certainly start to see why some of these people are paid so much.

Take Jack Welch, the former CEO of GE. He was a C plus student, a really second-rate student. He was once asked about the most important attribute he had. He said, "What really counts is that I'm Irish and I know how to tell stories." There's a lot of truth to that. When you tell stories to Wall Street, it has tremendous economic and financial implications. We can debate how useful it is. But it has large practical implications.

So these are some of the roads that I took to get to this subject. I'd encourage you to think about what role stories play in cultures, in organizations, in business, in the economy, in society. I think you'll find that story plays a much greater role than you'd find in any textbook on organizational life, on social life, or on cognitive life.

John Seely Brown: How I Came to Storytelling

Communicating Complexity

I got involved in storytelling in a different way.

One day about 8 years ago, I got a call from George Lucas, the filmmaker, and he said, "John, will you come up to the ranch and spend an afternoon with me? I'm doing a film on education and the future of education in the 21st century."

I looked at him and I said, "George, there's no way anybody's going to want to hear about this stuff."

So of course I went up there. He's an incredibly friendly, approachable guy, and we ended up talking for about 2 hours, face-to-face. A couple of other people were there. At some point, we were getting into some complex aspects of cognitive theory, and very esoteric material. I looked at him and I said, "George, there's no way anybody is going to want to hear about this stuff! No way!"

George Lucas looks at me and says, "John, perhaps you don't know, but most people consider me a pretty good storyteller."

There was a pregnant pause as I absorbed the meaning of what he was saying.

"John," he continued, "why don't you let me worry about that side of things. OK?"

This was a defining moment for me.

Learning to Work with the World

A second defining moment for me had occurred somewhat earlier. I was initially trained in theoretical mathematics and hard-core computer science. This moment showed me the extent to which a theoretical mathematician didn't fully understand how the world really works.

Before I started working for Xerox, I had been doing troubleshooting for the Air Force, building computer science systems as job-performance aids to help people to be more effective at troubleshooting. Then I joined Xerox, and after a while, they discovered my background.

So they said, "John, you really have to help us." In those days, most days, those machines broke down.

So I said, "You know, it would be helpful if I could meet some expert troubleshooters."

They said, "Fine, we've got a wonderful troubleshooter out in Leesburg, Virginia. Why don't you go there and meet him?"

I said, "Great."

They called in advance and told him that I was coming.

Well, my first mistake was that I walked into his office wearing a suit. This was not good.

He was the kind of guy who fixes real machines. Clearly he wasn't happy to see me. He was saying to himself, "Now here's a suit, and it's going to be a total loss. And he's an academic—even more of a loss. Clearly, he has his head high up in the sky. Now, how quickly can I get rid of him?"

And he looks at me, and he says, "John, this letter says that you're an expert troubleshooter. So I'm going to give you a little problem. Here's the problem. This is a relatively high-speed copier. And this copier has an intermittent copy-quality fault." Anybody who's done any trouble-shooting knows that an intermittent fault is nasty. If it's always broken, it doesn't take too much to figure it out. But if it's intermittent, it's tough.

So he says, "So John, this is The Official Xerox Procedure for fixing an Intermittent Quality Problem. It has five steps. You take this brilliantly conceived computer generated test pattern. And you put it on the platen." That's where normal people put the paper. We have a fancy term for everything. "Then you dial in, '5000 copies.' And you push the START button. Now you tell me, John, what do you do next?"

> Now here's a suit coming in, so it's going to be a total loss. And he's an academic—even more of a loss.

I said, "You get some coffee."

"Right."

So I scored one point. I can divide 50 pages (per minute) into 5000. I wasn't a total loss.

Then he said, "Yes, that's what you do. You go get some coffee. A few minutes. Maybe half an hour. Then you come back and the next step is to take this pile of 5000 copies, 10 reams of paper, and you plough through the pile until you find an example of something bad, and then you save that. And then you plough through the pile some more until you get to something else that's bad and you save that too. And that's how you do this, right?"

"Yes."

And then he said, "Well John, since you're an expert troubleshooter, surely you would have a better idea how to diagnose this machine, right? So why don't you tell me how you would go about doing it. Clearly you are cleverer than this rote procedure."

I hemmed and hawed and I tried to put off answering. The truth is that I was trying to get him to say something. It's an old trick in the Air Force. So for about 10 minutes, I danced around. Then he became impatient and he said, "Blah, blah, damn it, John, are you going to tell me how you'd do it, or not?"

And I said, "I'm sorry, Paul, I just can't think of anything." He stared at me. "I mean, I'd do something similar."

And he said, "I thought so!"

So I asked him, "Paul, how would you do it?"

And he looks at me and he says, "Surely it's obvious what to do!" He walks across the room to the waste basket next to the copier. He picks up the waste basket, and brings it over to a table, dumps the contents on the table, quickly sifts through the paper, and about thirty seconds later, comes up with brilliant sets of copy-quality problems. And he says, "You know, John, when someone discovers a copy-quality problem, do they classify it as a Copy Quality Problem? No. They classify it as a messed-up copy and they throw it away. So why don't you let the world do a little bit of the work for you? Why don't you work *with* the world, and see that there's a natural way to have the world collect this information for you. Just step back and read the world a little bit."

That phrase, "Read the world a little bit" is almost like judo.

> As I walked out, I thought to myself: this guy is a genius.

Paul said, "This waste basket was ready at hand. It was already there. It was already full of this stuff. Learn to work with the world, and you're going to find your life a lot simpler."

As I walked out, I thought to myself, "This guy is a genius." I also realized that it would be very hard to build computer systems that could do what Paul had just done.

So this was a major event for me. It was about the same time that I came across a book by Bruno Latour on *bricolage*.[4] That's an even better term for what we're talking about. This was a huge inspiration for me.

Communicating Rapidly

Then another thing happened having to do with the way an organization works. It turns out that one of the problems that CEOs have is: how do you communicate a message effectively throughout the entire corporation? So one day, I was in our CEO's office and he was talking about how hard it was to get a strategic message to everybody.

And I said, "You know, actually, I have no trouble at all doing that. In fact, I can get a message out in 48 hours, across the entire world of Xerox people. Tens of thousands of people in 28 countries."

> *I would have no trouble getting a message to everyone in Xerox in 48 hours.*

He looked amazed. "You can?"

"Yes, it's very simple." Now I was thinking back to Paul, and how he'd used the wastebasket. I said, "You know, there is something called the social fabric of an organization. You ought to see how fast I can spread a rumor about you in this corporation."

He looked at me strangely.

I continued. "A naturally occurring force happens in terms of spreading rumors throughout the social fabric. Is there not a way to tap that naturally occurring phenomenon in terms of how you spread an official message?"

Of course, rumors are rumors. But stories also live in the same social fabric. And they have their own trajectories, wonderful rapid trajectories through that same social space. And that turned out to be another major lesson for me about the force and potency of stories in organizations.

> *Stories have their own trajectories, wonderful rapid trajectories through the social fabric of the organization.*

STEVE DENNING: HOW I CAME TO STORYTELLING

For someone who is by nature quiet and introverted and certainly not given to natural loquacity, it's a surprise to find myself talking about storytelling at all. I am not a raconteur. I certainly didn't spend my youth telling stories. Nor did my family. They were equally taciturn. My schooling had taught me that storytelling was not important. And since then, my career had been based on being an analytical thinker, someone who could draw sharp distinctions and make crisp decisions.

For several decades, I was very successful in this mode as the quintessential analytical manager. In such a setting, with all this social reinforcement, it was natural for me to go on thinking that storytelling was not important. As recently as 5 years ago, I knew that storytelling was ephemeral, subjective, personal, indirect, and unscientific—all very bad things.

> *I knew that storytelling was ephemeral, subjective, personal, indirect, and unscientific—all very bad things.*

My personal discovery of the power of storytelling was thus not the result of a conscious search, or even any particular inclination toward storytelling. I stumbled upon the discovery because I was desperate to find a way to communicate a new idea to an organization where I had no hierarchical authority to back me up. I thought that my idea was good, and yet nobody was willing to listen. The standard forms of communication simply didn't work.

Then I came across an anecdote, and I used it in my presentations. It seemed to work a little. I tried more stories, and they worked even better. This evolution wasn't easy for me, since relying on storytelling meant jettisoning pretty much everything on which I had built my work and career up to that point.

Eventually I had the growing suspicion—which was thoroughly counter-intuitive to me—that storytelling was the only thing that was working for me when it came to explaining a complex idea to a difficult, resistant audience and getting them moving quickly into positive action.

My first stab at sharing the idea that storytelling might be significant was very tentative. I was at a conference in late 1997, and I happened to mention in passing during a presentation that perhaps storytelling was important in what I was doing. Immediately after the presentation, someone came up to me and proposed that I write a book.

"About what?" I asked.

She said, "About storytelling."

"But that's all I know," I said. "Perhaps storytelling is important."

"Don't worry," she said. "Just start writing."

I took the suggestion to heart, and I spent some time finding out more about narrative, trying to figure out why and how it was important. And I experimented further. The book that I ended up writing describes my journey of discovery and makes it available to others so that they could use it as a point of reference.[5]

When the book was published, it led to further interest in the subject and requests from individuals and organizations to tell them about storytelling and to teach them how to use it in their organizations. I had been using storytelling to generate organizational change, but now I also began exploring its use in other contexts and for other purposes, such as transferring knowledge, nurturing community, stimulating innovation, crafting communications, in education and training, and in preserving values. In fact, I started seeing storytelling and narrative everywhere I looked.

> *The thread had become so long that it could encircle the entire world.*

It was as though I had pulled on a short thread in a piece of fabric, and kept pulling until the thread had become so long that it could encircle the entire world. What seemed at first like a tiny and unpromising idea turned out to be something with massive ramifications. It was a huge surprise to me.

Katalina Groh: How I Came to Storytelling

A Family of Storytellers

I've been making films for 10 years. But it is just this past 6 months that I've created a film series called, "Real People, Real Stories[TM]," focusing on great teachers, leaders, anybody who is a good storyteller.

Getting into storytelling was a natural progression for me. Storytelling was part of my background from the moment I could talk. My parents are from Hungary. I was the only one of our family born in the United States. And home for my family is the dinner table.

In our family, we say that the stories get better with every new telling.

We don't now live in the same house where we grew up. So when we all come together, wherever that happens to be, we sit around a table and talk. We tell the same stories. We laugh. We have a terrific time. We take turns retelling the same stories until 2 or 3 in the morning.

In our family, we say that the stories get better with every new telling. That's why they are retold. And that's how I spent most of my childhood, just living and learning about our history, and our past, where I was from, and so on, through stories.

When I went to school, I studied finance and economics, and I decided to be a trader at the Chicago Board of Trade. I did that so that I could travel, 2 or 3 months out of the year. I had a lot of freedom. I could paint and take photographs and that was a different form of storytelling, because every painting I made was a story. So I was living my life, going to work, but my life was really about creating stories.

My Entry into Film-making

Then one day, almost by accident, I was asked through some friends to work on an independent feature film that came to Chicago. I accepted. I was thinking that this would be interesting. I might learn something new.

But the first day I was there, I knew that something had happened. I was entranced by the collaborative process of making a film. I knew at once that that's what I wanted to do. And that's how I got into making films.

And over the next 6 months, I learned about the process of 150 people working together to create a film. The bad part was that the film itself was not good. We were making a low-budget action feature film. It was with gangs—real gangs in the streets of Chicago. The only thing that we were really teaching in that film was showing children how to kill each other. It was a bad film, but we sold it even before we finished making it—a sad commentary on our society.

After that first film, I began making documentaries. About 6 years ago I was hired by the CEO of New World Entertainment. He was looking to create a new division, an educational division, called World Knowledge. And he wanted to try something different. In fact, when he offered me the job, I told him, "I don't make educational films."

But he said, "No, but you tell stories. You tell very good stories."

So he went completely outside of the market to find somebody who liked to tell stories.

Making a film is an ongoing learning process for my company, and we have a lot of fun doing it. One of the first things I learned in creating reality-based educational films is that people recall something when they hear it told within a story. We found that people remembered the story. The more we work on making educational films, the more we realize that it's really about creating experiences, through telling stories.

> *People recall something when they hear it told within a story.*

Chapter Endnotes

[1] Donald (Deirdre) McCloskey, Arjo Klamer, (1995) One Quarter of GDP is Persuasion (in Rhetoric and Economic Behavior) *The American Economic Review*, Vol. 85, No. 2, page 195.

[2] ibid.

[3] Source: World Bank development indicators.

[4] *Laboratory Life*, by Bruno Latour, Steve Woolgar, Jonas Salk. Princeton University Press. 1986.

[5] *The Springboard: How Storytelling Ignites Action in Knowledge-Era Organizations*, by Stephen Denning (Butterworth Heinemann, Boston, 2000).

TWO
Storytelling in Organizations

Economists view talk as cheap and culture as insignificant. Yet human beings are talking animals ... The talk probably matters. Why else would the human animals bother doing it?

—Deirdre McCloskey[1]

Larry Prusak's Original Presentation

CATEGORIES OF STORIES IN ORGANIZATIONS

Let's talk about stories in organizations. When people talk about story, what is it that they are talking about? We can categorize the stories people tell in a number of ways.

If we were to put a microphone in every coffee station, every doorway, every stairwell in the Global 1000 firms and we collected all the stories told over a month and categorized them, what would these stories be about?

> When people tell stories in organizations, what exactly are they talking about?

Stories about Other People

In the first place, we'd find that they're telling stories about other people. The stories are about co-workers, other people who work in the organization. Why do people tell stories about their co-workers? Malicious gossip is a fairly small category. Not many people tell a story to harm somebody, like telling a salacious or malicious story about someone's behavior. That's not done very much. There are people who do it, mischievous people, but it's not done that often.

What researchers have found is that when people tell stories about other people, the motivations are reliability, trust and knowledge.[2] People want to know: is this person reliable? If he says "x," will x occur? If she says that she'll do something, will she do it? Reliability. When you tell stories about another person, it tells them: "That guy promised this," or "She did that." That's some of the great storytelling content: reliability.

And reliability is a good first cousin, if not a sibling, to trust. Eighteen books have been published on the subject in the last 3 years.[3] Trust is important. Nothing of value will happen without trust, because without trust you have to negotiate and contract and monitor everything, so that you never get to the content and no substance gets done. You constantly have your nose up someone else's you know what. Trust is key. And when people tell stories about other people, they're often about this: can you trust this person?

And there's a third category. When people talk about people, it is sometimes called gossip. Jim March at Stanford wrote a great piece about this: gossip is just news about people that you need to know. How else would you know if someone is trustworthy, knowledgeable or reliable? If someone says, "So and so is trustworthy," I may trust the person who tells me that, and that's a proxy, one step away. But often, you want more. Often you tell me a story about this person. "This person said he'd do this, and he did that." You could say that they're gossiping, but you could also say that they're informing others of vital news. They're spreading information about the person's expertise, reliability, and trustworthiness. This is significant stuff.

So when you see people chatting with one another, and you overhear them talking about some other person, they're really exchanging news, news about other people's reliability. This is important especially as organizations become more virtual and more volatile. Since there's less physical space, they don't meet so often.

People now work in odd places. Some firms have bought a lot of non-sense about virtuality. They say you don't need offices or you don't need places to meet. This is mainly untrue, stuff put out by IT vendors. It's untrue, but people believe it and so it succeeds in selling IT.

- If you don't have physical space and you never meet people, how are you going to know if they're reliable?
- If you put them on a team, how will you know if they would perform?
- How will you know whether you want them on a team?
- How do you know how to work with them?
- How can you do any of these things without telling a story? Or without hearing stories about them?

People say: "Well, that's very unscientific." But what's the alternative? Are there any? How else would you know about a person? There aren't any alternatives. You have to get it through a story.

Let me give you an example. I know two people. There's Steve Denning who worked at the World Bank, and there's Dave Snowden who works for me at IBM. They do storytelling workshops together. I had to convince each of them that the other person was trustworthy. And there's a good reason for that. You don't want to go half way round the world doing a seminar with someone unless you trust that person. They'd heard of each other's reputation, and they trusted me enough, so it worked out. But it's still one step away.

People might say, "What are you doing, Larry? Are you telling stories?"

My reply is, "Yes, that's right. I'm telling stories." You tell stories about the other person. "They showed up. They did this. They didn't hog all the time. They were careful on this and that."

What are the alternatives to telling stories? There aren't any. No system can do it. No human resource department can do it. There's nothing else but stories. So that's an important category: stories about people. You can call it gossip. But again, it's very rarely malicious. It's news. Ezra Pound said, "Poetry is news that stays news." And sometimes gossip and rumors are news that stay news. They have great endurance.

Stories about the Work Itself

Re-engineering was one of those great tsunamis that attack organizations and often kill them.

The second thing that people talk about is stories about the work itself, about the nature of the work. How to do it better? How to do it at all?

Dave Snowden, who works for me at IBM, has a wonderful tale about the Thames Water Authority. This organization does the water and the pipes for the Thames Valley. The company had been re-engineered.

Re-engineering is a terrible thing. It was a wave that swept over various parts of the world, but it was based on very faulty assumptions, and almost ruined a number of companies. It was one of those great tsunamis that attack organizations and almost kill them. Re-engineering was the latest of those efficiency waves that run people and organizations into the dust.

The Thames Water Authority had beautiful handwritten records of the homes where people lived along the river, and the water pipes that brought the water into their houses. The pipes were from the 19th century. Under re-engineering, the consultants had said, "That's 19th century stuff. We don't need that. We're going to put it all on a system." So they took these beautiful 19th century handwritten books and destroyed them. And they put the information on a system that didn't work.

So when workmen went to someone's home, they couldn't access the pipes, and they had to re-create the handwritten records. The workmen had to get together and try to find people who remembered where the pipes were. It was very tactile, tacit, contextual knowledge. The workmen had to re-create the whole thing.

So they'd meet and have coffee every morning and they'd say: "Which house are you going to?"

"Ah. I think John used to know about that one. Give him a call."

John would say, "Oh yes, when you do this, it's copper and it leads into this."

These are stories about the work itself. There's a famous book by Julian Orr called *Talking about Machines.*[4] It tells how the Xerox Corporation in its rationalist mode put out enormous documentation on fixing these big high-speed copiers. You can imagine the huge volumes of procedures and standards. Orr's book is about the Xerox Corporation, but it could be about IBM or any other company. They do exactly the same thing. It turns out the repairmen just talk to each other. When they have a problem, they call each other up. When the company gave them mobile phones, that made it even easier. It works. Why?

First, because it's much easier to understand another person talking about a subject than it is to read any documentation.

Secondly, because you don't know what problems you're going to find until you find them.

And thirdly, because a lot of learning occurs in the interaction between the people.

"Did you try this?"

"That didn't work?"

"Well how about this?"

"Maybe you should try that."

You do verbal decision trees in the form of stories. That's how most people help each other at work. They tell stories about the work.

Julian Orr's book is an ethnographic study showing exactly how people tell stories about the work. John Seely Brown will discuss it in more detail.

Is talk about the work useful?

Alan Webber, the founder of Fast Company, once wrote an article with the title, "Stop Talking and Get Back to Work." It's one of the dumbest things ever said in American business. And there's a lot of competition for that title. There are very low barriers to entry.

And there's a former CEO of IBM, John Akers. When IBM was in deep distress, really in trouble, he went up to Canada and spoke. He blamed the workers for hanging around the water coolers instead of focusing on their jobs. That was about the worst thing he could have said. First, it was immoral for someone taking that sort of salary to be blaming the workers for the problems of the firm. And second, it was stupid. What do you think people are going to do when a firm is in distress? They're going to talk to each other. They're going to tell stories. They're going to try to help dig the firm out of whatever problems it's gotten into. They'll try to come up with local solutions. To help their offices as best they can. To help their branch. To help their division. The very worst thing you could tell people is not to talk to their fellow workers when there are grave problems like that.

And what we're really talking about here is a different mental model of how an organization works. I'm talking about a non-mechanistic non-rationalist model, a model that is organic and self-adjusting, where people talk to each other and things are not as crisp, or as clear, or as rational, or as scientific as they appear in the mechanistic models. Organizations don't function like a machine. Organizations have a lot of people in them. And what do the people do? They talk to each other about the work, mostly in the form of stories.

What about the classroom?

Some people suggest that the idea that talking is bad may have its origins in old-style classroom practices where young children were not supposed to talk. Sometimes as you get older, you get pessimistic and think that the world is going to the dogs. But when I talk to kids, I can see that their classrooms are much better than mine were. The kids walk around and talk to each other. They certainly learn more. I grew up in schools where you were supposed to be sitting there and you couldn't say a word. I was a chatty inquisitive kid and it was murder for me. I hated it. It was a miserable experience.

Children are naturally chatty and inquisitive. Every now and then you have to say: "Hey, be quiet and listen." But basically, it's crazy to try to keep them quiet for 7 or 8 hours a day.

It's possible that John Akers, the IBM executive, grew up in that model. He was a navy guy. The old navy! Those were straitlaced people who thought you should sit still and listen. The training models in most firms are still based on this approach. It's the Monty Python theory of learning: you open up someone's head, pour in some knowledge. Total nonsense.

If we think about how we first learn, we realize that we first learn through stories. And we continue in this mode, learning first through those initial stories that we hear from our parents, our brothers and sisters, our friends, and so forth, and that first imprint stays with us throughout life, as research shows.[5] It's storytelling and adaptation and looking. All of those things are more ecological and organic than the models we use for training or formal classroom teaching methods.

Distinguishing Dialogue, Conversation, and Story

Some people would argue that there's a difference between dialogue, conversation, and story. For our purposes here, I don't see the difference as significant. There's academic literature on discourse analysis. People have developed methodologies for analyzing conversations—sociologists, and ethnographic researchers. There are ways to understand what goes on between two people, or three people, or a group, for example, by analyzing and looking at how they speak. Erving Goffman[6] and Harold Garfinkel[7] have written about that. It's academic writing, but it's interesting. For our purposes, we're just saying: loosen the screws. Loosen the couplings. Let people talk to each other, and they'll learn a lot about what goes on in their organization and help make the organization work.

Stories about the Organization

Then there are stories about the organization.

If you want a great example of this, let me tell you a true-life story. There was once a company called Chemical Bank. It merged into another bank. And then yet again, became a third bank. But at the time of this story, it was a big powerful New York bank called the Chemical Bank. And they had a new Chief Information Officer named Bruce Hassenjager. He was a powerful guy, an IT guy, a smart guy. He looked at the systems that the bank was always building, and he said, "Let's try something different."

He knew that a lot of people were worried about what was going on, since this was the era when the banks were merging with one another. There were rumors going around. So he said, "Why don't we put up a system called RumorMill?" It was an IT system called RumorMill. Harvard Business School has written a case about it.

He said, "In this system, if you type in a rumor, I'll get you an answer in 24 hours." You'd send it to him, via the system. It wasn't quite e-mail. It was just before e-mail, but you'd use it like e-mail.

When he first let people know that this system was up, he got about five inquiries. And he sent answers back to them. He was an executive. He was on the management team. So he was able to get answers.

People could see that the system was reliable and reasonably honest. So the next week he got about 100 inquiries. He could batch some of them together. They weren't all separate questions. You could imagine the sort of questions he'd receive:

"Are we merging with Chase?"

"I heard we're going to go bankrupt. Is it true?"

"Are we getting a new CEO?"

He answered most of them, though he had to get one of his people to help him. But he managed to get answers to most of the questions. Sometimes he couldn't. Sometimes he had to say, "Look, I'm sorry, I'm afraid this is still secret information. I really can't answer it." That was fine. People could live with that.

The next week, he got 4000 inquiries. And he had to shut the system down, and after a few months he left the firm.

What's interesting about that experience is the evidence of the bottled-up need for information. Here is a bank being run on the traditional models, having all the traditional systems, with a pent-up demand for information about their own organization that was so huge that it swamped the system and it swamped Bruce. That's true for every organization. Maybe less true than it used to be. But if you did something like that in IBM or GE or GM or the Navy or any large organization, the same thing would occur. People don't know what's going on. So they tell stories. In this case, it was a veritable Delphic Oracle. You could ask a question and get an authoritative answer. It's on a screen. It's from an executive. People said: "Wow! This is great stuff!"

How much of that was due to the illusion, or even the fact, of anonymity? Not much. People just wanted to know. They were curious. Carl Weick wrote a wonderful book called *Sensemaking in Organizations*.[8] He said that the strongest impulse in many organizations is to make sense of the organization and the environment. It's not the total truth, but it's a big piece of it. People want to make sense of their own organizations.

So these are stories about the organization. Not about the work, but about the organization that you work in. You know the subjects.

"How did that jerk get promoted?"

"Why did the stock price go through the floor?"

"Where has our pension gone?"

I find this myself. I'm an executive in IBM at a senior level, and yet I have to read the newspapers to find out what goes on in IBM. No one tells me. I read the newspaper and I see: "Oh, we bought this firm! We did that? How fascinating!"

I'm a stockholder and a stakeholder in IBM, but somehow they can't get the news to me. I once met the Senior Vice President for Communications, and I asked him, "What the hell do you do for a living?" He was deeply offended. He outranked me by two degrees, so he wouldn't answer. I'm not singling out IBM. It's a good firm. It would be the same in any large firm.

So people love telling stories about their organization, and not from maliciousness. A related impulse is to retain your buddies. People want to keep their networks and communities intact. People tell stories to retain other people in the organization that they want to keep there. Researchers are now coming to more community-based or network-based theory of the firm. A number of us have written about it.[9] Firms are social communities, and it's very important to keep these communities intact to get coherence and cohesion. So when people tell stories about the organization, it's often a bonding mechanism.

The Context of the Story

It's also important to note that stories need a context. Stories are told at a particular time and at a particular place. There are times when you may have a story and not want to tell it, and then, later on, you find the time when you do want to tell it. "Ripeness is all" as Shakespeare said.[10] Timing is important.

There are certain timeless stories. If you were to do discourse analysis and collected all the stories told in every organization in the world for 5 years, you'd find there are timeless stories. Stories like, "Us against them" or "I do all the work around here" or "The reward is disproportionate to the effort." These are tales or myths or legends that are perennial in organizations. You find them in Hammurabi's code.[11] You find them in the Bible. You find them in the Iliad and the Odyssey. There are probably six or eight eternal themes. They're timeless.

Then there are contextual stories, stories that are true for the moment. Like the RumorMill at Chemical Bank. Stories about what constantly goes on in organizations. "So and so was promoted." Or "Someone else was let go." There is constant tension between eternal tales, which are stories like "Woe is me!" and stories relevant to a particular context.

> As Shakespeare said in King Lear, "Ripeness is all."

Stories as Social Bonding

There are also stories that are told for social bonding. You've probably been an observer when people get together for a meeting in a large firm like IBM or Xerox, and they start out telling stories before they get to the business of the meeting. Often they'll piss and moan about the firm for a little bit. It's known as ritualistic speech.

People need to do that before they can talk about what's on the formal agenda of the meeting. It's not wildly different from praying. It's using speech to bond people together. "We have a common goal. We have a common objective. We're all treated the same. Now we can trust each other." It's like sacrificing a goat. They probably could do that with the same motivation and get the same result. I'm only half joking.

There's a wonderful phrase used by anthropologists called *phatic speech*. Here it's not the content that matters, but the fact that you're saying it to bond with another person. You're doing it as a ritual. It's like saying: "How are you?" to someone. It's a phatic statement. You may not really give a damn. It means: "I acknowledge your presence."

The talk at the start of the meeting usually signifies: "Let's get together. We all trust each other. Here's who we are. We're people who are pissed off because we work in this firm and these things occurred and this is how we feel." And then we can get into the content of the meeting.

Some people even argue that that language doesn't just describe reality, but it actually creates reality, and that when people complain about how badly things are going, they are actually creating the negativity in the environment. There's a certain amount of truth to this. Persistent negativism can sink a firm. But usually there are also hard economic realities underlying the complaints. You can't look at organizations and understand what's going on in them outside of their economic context.

Language alone doesn't create reality. For a lot of people, it is unfair to be working the way they are working in organizations. When you see the disproportion of reward to effort, or when people lose their job or

> *You go into a company and you can read the signals from the architecture or the way the desks are laid out. You ask yourself, like Corday in the Marat Sade, "What sort of place is this?"*

their pension or both, or when the working conditions are difficult, you can see that working life can be really hard for some people. The economics of it largely determine the outcome.[12] Personally I'm treated well, but for others, there are usually real reasons for people to be upset. Often stories are outlets for these feelings. I am less of a social constructionist than others. I'm more of an economist.

Stories as Signals

Stories about organizations also serve as signals. Many stories told about organizations can be classified as signal interpretation. Call it hermeneutics if you like fancy language. Reading the signs. Interpreting what they mean.

I was a consultant for many years, and consultants after a while hone their skills through experience. If you go into a company as a consultant, you read all sorts of signs, like the architecture. The way desks are laid out. The configuration of offices. And everyone reads the signs. It tells you what sort of organization this is.

There's a play called the *Marat-Sade*.[13] And Corday, one of the characters, comes to Paris and asks, "What sort of a place is this?" In the same way, people in organizations ask themselves: "What sort of a company is this?" Now people might say that's unscientific. But I generally found that it was pretty accurate. I'd check things out with the people who actually worked in the firm and ask them what it was like. Usually they'd say, "Yes, this firm really is that way." So then I'd know that I wasn't way off-base when I was reading the signs.

Architecture Can Tell Stories

Stories don't have to be expressed in words to have a narrative thrust. There are other kinds of stories. Architecture can tell stories. The configuration of office space tells stories. Take Harvard Business School. It's a place with a great deal of money, almost more money than God. Yet they put up a new building, Shad Hall, for the faculty, where there is absolutely no public space. Every person has a private office. When you want to meet people, you have to meet outside the building, because when you go in, it's just offices and columns. Now occasionally the professors have to meet with consultants. So eventually they forced the dean to put in a little coffee stand in the lobby. It's a tiny place. Otherwise people had absolutely nowhere to go. There was no common space. Now that's a tremendous signal that Harvard is sending to anyone who comes into that building. Here they are, trying to teach teamwork in organizations. And there was no common space. So architecture is a story also. Buildings act as signs and information about the organization. It's a very interesting subject.

Stories about the Past

Another category is that of stories about the past. The history of organizations. This often bounds people. Stories about the past constrain a lot of behavior in organizations. These stories can have such power that economists call it path-dependency, meaning that the road you took determines where you are going. But when economists talk about it, they usually don't explain what exactly in the past makes a firm path-dependent. They don't get into the actual mechanism of how that works. Stories play a very big role here.

Take IBM for example. I was on a number of committees, acquisition committees, and very often in these discussions someone would say: "We tried that and it didn't work." Now, what they said was true. We had tried it and it hadn't worked. And that didn't mean that it would never work. But the story they were telling and the way they were telling it bounded the behavior. It constrained behavior. It was as though they were saying, "The Bishop wills it" or "God wills it."

You hear this all the time, maybe in different versions.

"We tried that and it didn't increase sales in Germany."

"You can't open an office in Kuala Lumpur."

"You can't acquire a telecom firm."

IBM tried three times to buy a telecom firm, and each time it was a disaster. Does that mean necessarily that the fourth time it will also be a disaster? Not at all. There is no logic behind it. But the story is powerful, and it becomes embedded in legends and myths. There are opportunity costs since people's careers were killed because they did this. The associations of the story become so powerful that it constrains behavior, often to the detriment of what could be done. The story itself becomes a very powerful factor.

It's like telling a child, "God is always watching you! If you do something bad, you will go to hell!" It certainly influences the child, usually not for the better. I used to hear things like that when I was growing up.

There's an implicit message in the story, but making it explicit doesn't seem to help. You'd think it would change things, but it doesn't. So even if the kid reads Bertrand Russell when he's older and discovers that there is no God, he will probably still feel funny. He may feel that way all his life.

Stories thus promote cultural norms. That's one of the ways that norms get transferred. If you're interested in norms, the best book written about this is *Social Norms*.[14] It explains how norms in organizations grow, how they evolve, where they are. I don't think norms develop from stories, but stories carry lessons about behavior. Stories say, "Do this, not that!" That establishes and helps these norms to be perpetuated within organizations.

The Unreliable Story

The story gained tremendous credence, and most people still think that it's true.

A lot of research has shown that stories evolve over time. The stories become socially constructed to reflect additional viewpoints or changes in viewpoint. It's what Carl Weick called "retrospective sensemaking." You change an opinion, and suddenly the story itself changes.

There's a well-known example from Honda. For years, the story was told about the Honda company. It was put into a case format by the Harvard Business School. Stories gain cognitive authority when institutions pick them up and circulate them. Harvard Business School is in the business of cognitive authority. They say, "This is true. It has Harvard's seal of approval." And people will accept that it's true. So there was this story about Honda, about how Honda wiped out Harley-Davidson in the motorcycle wars, at least for a while. Harley obviously came back. And there were certain things that Honda did with market research and so forth. Then one day, Richard Pascale, a business researcher, looked into it and found it that it wasn't true.[15] There was chance, luck, circumstances, a whole set of things, what Jim March called the *Garbage Can Model of Decisions*.[16] Everything was thrown into the can. The can was shaken up. Something came out. And Honda won some market share. It was not the result of rational decision-making, even though the Japanese were very rational in what they tried to do. And yet the story gained tremendous credence. Even after Pascale showed that it wasn't true, most people still think that it's true. And a lot of stories are like that. As John Seely Brown says in the next chapter, once we think we know something, it's hard to unlearn what we think we know.

Oral Histories of Organizations

People sometimes ask me how to approach writing an oral history of an organization. What should they do and what shouldn't they do? Sometimes I tell them what Voltaire said about history. "It's a pack of tricks played on the dead." If you can find people still alive who were around when the organization was created and who can really talk about it, my advice is to interview these people and tape the conversations on video. Talk to people who have stories to tell, and let the viewers make their own decision as to what this means. I usually advise them not to write it. There are firms that write histories for other firms. But almost no one reads them, because we know they are not true. It doesn't accord with our own sense of how an organization would work. Country histories are different. Professional historians often write really well and honestly, and readers agree that, yes, that must have been the way it was. But corporate histories are different. I've read a number of them. They're mostly public relations, that is to say, bunk, and people know it. So I'd recommend interviewing people and letting them talk. Then others can watch the tapes and make up their own minds as to what they mean.

Stories about the Future

Then there are stories about the future. This is where mission and vision statements fit in. They are saying: "This is what we'd like to be."

Or: "Here's what we're aspiring to be."

Or: "Here's what we're going to be in the future."

Or: "We're going to be a great firm."

Or: "We're going to rise up from the dead."

We all tell stories about the future. You can call it different things. You might call it "religion." You might call it "child-rearing." But these are stories about the future. We tell prescriptive stories about the way life is going to be.

When I was a Ph.D. student, I studied with a man who was a great authority on utopian visions, and utopian societies, and the two sides of it—how that often leads to some terrible horrors. Some of them were in the 20th century. Some were in other centuries. But there's a real perennial need for people to have some vision of a better land. A better future. That somehow in the future, things will be OK. The lion will lay down with the lamb. Woody Allen said, "That could happen, but the lamb wouldn't get a lot of sleep."

Maybe the lion will lay down with the lamb. But as Woody Allen pointed out, it could happen but the lamb wouldn't get much sleep.

These are stories about the future. We all tell them. We all need to hear them. Who could live without them? Could anyone go through life having no stories about the future? No planned script in your head about the future? I don't think so.

And that's what mission statements are. They're not evil. They're not intending to deceive. They fulfill real needs by pointing the way forward.

Using Stories to Spark Change and Shed Old Stories

People sometimes ask me what are the chances within an organization of creating a story about the future that people will really buy into? And how long does that take? One answer is to go and look at the World Bank. Steve Denning actually did that at the World Bank. It's interesting, because now we have a detailed rich case of someone who has done this and studied it and written about it.[17] Steve will talk about this in Chapter 4.

Getting Beyond Stories of the Past

We've talked about stories of the future. But often there are people who hold on to the stories about the past, and so one never gets to the stories about the future. People say: "You can't do this. We tried it and it didn't work." People often ask: how do you get beyond that?

One answer is: get rid of the people who tell those stories. They will retire. They will die. Now those may sound like flip answers, but these stories can have devastating consequences. Go to the Middle East, or the Balkans, or Ireland, and you'll hear people tell terrible stories about the past. Where I grew up, I kept hearing stories about what occurred in World War II and who did what to whom. These stories were telling me: "Don't trust whole classes of people and countries. Don't trust any of them!"

I thought to myself: "How could that be? There are 70 million of these people. How could you not trust any of them?"

But they were very strong stories, and they were told with feeling and guts and blood and murder. So they had a terrific impact. It was hard to overcome this. I remember the first time I went to a country that I had been told by my parents and other relatives was full of murderers. Even though I knew that it was nonsense and even madness—these people weren't even alive during World War II—it still had an impact on me. I still felt nervous. I couldn't help myself, even though I like to think I'm a fairly rational person. Those stories were strong.

Think of Serbs telling stories about Turks. Turks telling stories about Greeks. Greeks telling stories about Turks. Albanians telling stories about Serbs. Serbs telling stories about Croats. These stories go back to the 14th century. And they're resonant. Palestinians telling stories about Jews. Jews telling stories about Arabs.

I've been to Ireland, and I heard over and over again stories about the viciousness of the English. The English tell stories about the viciousness of other people. This stuff resonates. So it's a real dilemma in human life. Edmund Burke once said, "How can you indict a whole people?" The truth is that we do it all the time. And it's done in the form of stories. It certainly constrains peace-keeping missions. You can ask the people who are doing the killing, "Why are you killing those people? What is it about them?" The answers will be in the form of a story. Stories that are resonant with blood and death have great salience.

One Solution: Go Somewhere Else

One way to overcome the stories of the past is simply to leave. If it's a country, you may be able to emigrate. If it's an organization, it's usually easier and you can just switch jobs. It's a great way to break free. When you change jobs, you get a honeymoon period, just like the newly elected U.S. president. So if you're feeling very constrained, just go somewhere else and you'll probably get a honeymoon. In any event, the stories won't affect you for a while. There will inevitably be stories in your new environment, but at first you won't know them well enough to be affected by them.

Stories about Life Itself

Another category comprises stories about life itself.

Now I'm not an expert on life itself. In fact, I'd say that I'm probably deficient in knowledge in this area, given the way my own life has turned out. But very often, stor-

> *The workplace is where people learn about life.*

ies in organizations are about life, about children, about spouses, about love, about death, about parents.

It's another category. People learn about life through stories. You can read Ann Landers. You can buy books about it. But most people talk about the issues in their lives. Again, it's not being self-dramatizing or narcissistic. It's more about getting information, about aging parents, or about children with issues, or about matters of love and marriage, or whatever. I don't think this category should be ignored or dismissed. The workplace has become a place where people learn about life. It's where most people live their lives these days. The workplace has in many ways replaced the commons, the church, the community, the places we used to look for those sort of answers, as Bob Putnam has written.[18]

So people view the workplace as a place where you can learn about life rather more than the other venues where they used to learn this. In the past, people would just go to work and come home and then talk to their neighbors. Or talk on the green. Or talk at church. Or talk in some civic association. That seems to be waning. So the workplace becomes the place where people talk and learn about life through the stories that they hear.

Stories about Oneself: Identity

Another category comprises stories that I tell myself about me. Wittgenstein, the great philosopher, once said, "When you talk to yourself, who exactly is talking to whom?"

> *Wittgenstein said, "When you talk to yourself, who exactly is talking to whom?*

Nevertheless, presenting one's identity, presenting one's work identity, is important.

Often it's not just a matter of presenting it, but also consolidating it. The kinds of stories I tell myself about myself, in terms of what I have to live up to, or live down, or whatever—have a great bearing on my sense of identity. Most people act and then tell stories about their actions. They rarely construct a narrative and then act. They do things and then retrospectively make sense of it and present it that way. There is a lot of literature on the psychology of memory and identity.[19] I tend to spend more time with the literature on economic and social behaviors just from my own training and inclination. Not that one literature is better than the other. The great issue in social science is that no one has made the micro-macro link effective. What exactly are the ties between the economy and the social norms in society as a whole to individual psychology? It's never been done to universal satisfaction. But it's interesting comparing the different streams of thinking about it.

Electronic Storytelling

There's a lot of talk these days about electronic storytelling. I'm afraid I haven't experienced much of it myself. I've heard people say that they tell and hear stories through e-mail. But I find it hard to believe. I don't see stories in my e-mails. I hear them through talking to people. I must get 50 or 60 e-mails a day. Most of them are insipid. They are quick. We're all in a hurry and we get too many of them. We usually answer with five or six words. E-mail is not too different from writing. It's a quicker way of writing letters. It's like the telephone. It helps you communicate. It's useful in a mundane kind of way.

Telecommuting

People often ask me about telecommuting. Telecommuting is an accountant's dream, but it has a problem: it doesn't work. Why? There are two books with the same title, one in cognitive science and another book, a novel. Their title is *Being There*.[20] They help explain why telecommuting doesn't work. The point is, if you're not there, you're nowhere. No one has ever gotten promoted through tele-commuting. You don't get anywhere in the organization if you're telecommuting. You're out of loops. You're lonely. In IBM which believes in this big-time—sometimes people say the initials I-B-M stand for "I'm by myself"—it's a terrible way to work.

> *The point is, if you're not there, you're nowhere.*

Now from time to time, I work at home, for instance, if it snows or if I have a lot of writing to do. I'm not talking about periodically staying at home and finishing a project. I'm talking about having no office to go to. Having no space that's your own. Either you're on the road all the time, or you're with a laptop at a client site. You never talk to your co-workers. The organization learns nothing. You learn nothing. You're just a transaction. It's a stupid way to work. It's part of the technological utopianism that is now so thoroughly integrated with accounting methods. And it destroys once-great organizations.

It's no secret that I don't agree with the IBM management on this issue. They really believe in it. They do it for retention of employees. We can't get software writers unless we let them live in, say, Missoula, Montana. But IBM doesn't learn anything that way. You pay them on a transaction basis. It's tempting to do it, but nobody learns. You don't learn from the great coders because you never meet them. They don't learn anything because they don't meet the clients. They just do a job. They don't refresh their knowledge. So personally, I think it's a very poor way to work.

Why Do People Travel to Meetings?

The truth of the matter is, if you're not there, you're nowhere. I take the shuttle flight constantly between Boston and New York. There's a shuttle. It starts at 6 a.m. and it ends at 10 p.m. I've been on all of them. You get to know the same people. People nod or say hello. "Hi, how are you?" For the most part, they're tired, white, fat males.

But one day in 1999, I am waiting in Boston to get on that shuttle, and my cell phone rings. It's 6 a.m. Very few people have my number, but my wife does. And it's my wife. She's just been woken up and she's fairly ticked off. A client has called her, and told her that my meeting in New York has been cancelled. Somebody is ill. My wife is nice enough to call me and say, "You don't have to get on that plane."

> You get to know the same people. "Hi, how are you?" They're all tired, white, fat men mostly.

Great! It's 6 a.m. I can go to work at 6 a.m. It's early but I don't really mind. Not being on a plane is a day in heaven to me.

But I decide to do something different. After all, it really is too early to go to the office. So I do something that I wanted to do for years. I ask these people where the hell they are going. I have a suit on and a tie. I'm pretty harmless looking. I say, "Hi. How are you? I'm Larry Prusak. I'm with IBM. Would you mind telling me where you're going?"

> Not being on a plane is a day in heaven to me.

Some people know who I am.

Others say, "What? IBM? Are you selling something?"

And I say, "No, I just want to know where you're going."

About half the people are going to internal meetings. And they are from organizations that have all the communications technology that money could buy. These are the big mutual funds, the big biotech companies, the big hospitals, the big universities. You name the technology and they already have it.

So I ask them. "How come you're going to a meeting? You have all this technology. How come you're getting on this plane. It's early. It's expensive. It's a pain in the butt. New York City gives you a headache. Two expensive taxi rides. The driver's a maniac. Your blood pressure goes through the roof. You come home. You're dirty, hot, and tired. This is not a pleasurable experience. You have e-mail and all this video-conferencing. So why are you getting on planes, spending money and time. Why are you doing all this?"

They'd usually say something like, "Well, I just have to be there."
"But why?" I'd keep probing. "Why?"
"Well," they'd say, "if I'm not there something terrible will happen to me."
"What do you mean?" I'd say. "You're a senior-ish person."
"No, no! I have to be at the meeting, because I have to see other people's reaction."

The best answer I got was from someone who said, "You're from New York, right? You ever play hide and seek, and all those tag games? And you remember one kid who was always 'It'? Well, if you're not at the meeting, then you're going to be 'It'!"

That was the best answer I got. The truth is that people will move heaven and earth and fly around the world to be at the meeting, because they're worried they're going to be 'It.'

You can talk about lack of trust and that's some of it. But it's also about reading cues. Reading the signals. Reading emotions. Getting a cognitive sense of what's going on. Getting a sense of the social dynamic. This isn't replicable through today's technology. People say: what about the future? I don't know about the future. You can tell stories about the future. John Seely Brown is more hopeful than I am. But in any event, it isn't true today. Those planes are still full.

> *The truth is that people will move heaven and earth and fly around the world to be at the meeting, because they're worried they're going to be 'It.'*

In fact, human beings still need to see each other. Terrible things happen when people are not together.

Web Communities

Some people would say in defense of distributed-ness, that there are many thousands of vibrant virtual communities on the web. They say that there are hundreds of thousands of people that play in virtual environments and know and trust each other and develop their own communities. My own take on the situation is that it depends on how you define words like "know" and "trust" and "community". It's a judgment call in the end. But most people won't trust other people to the extent of really talking about serious things, not just the gross national product (GNP) of Morocco or regression analysis, but subjects needing real trust. People won't share this unless they know the other person. And it's hard to know others if you haven't met them. Some people say it's generational. And that may be so to a certain extent.

DIVERSITY IN STORYTELLING: GENDER, ETHNICITY, AND GENERATION

Gender Differences

People ask me whether there are significant differences in the workplace between the way women and men tell stories. When it comes to men and women, I don't think so. The differences between men and women in terms of narrative have been overstated and exaggerated.[21]

Differences in Ethnic Groupings

But between different cultural and ethnic groups, there are big differences. I grew up in a rich ethnic stew in Brooklyn, New York. You couldn't find a richer ethnic stew. Maybe parts of Chicago would equal that. Or Los Angeles. The people I grew up with were Jews, Italians, Irish, and blacks. These were the groups I was raised with. And these groups loved telling stories. These are all verbal cultures. And the groups were one neighborhood away from each other. These were all working class people. But they all believed in telling stories. They sometimes told long involved tales of family intrigue or stories of discrimination.

I remember one summer, getting a job at a very different place, an ad agency in New York City. It was run by different types of people who didn't tell stories. It felt very different. Maybe they told them at Harvard Club over a few martinis. But they didn't tell stories at work.

And you could really feel the difference in cultures. That may be changing.

Differences in Generations

Do different generations tell stories differently? I don't think so. We are wired this way. This is what human beings are like. There are certain changes here and there, a little movement, but people learn and live through stories and metaphors and connections. That's the sort of animal we are. Dogs sniff each other. Human beings tell stories. In terms of difference between groups, I think the strongest of the three categories—gender, ethnicity, and generations—would be ethnicity, the sort of cultural bearings that you pick up when you're younger.

The Homogenizing Impact of Television

What's really homogenizing us is television. I didn't watch much television when I was growing up, because there wasn't much television to watch. Television homogenizes the way that people speak about their activities. People make cultural references to television shows, which is hard on people who don't watch those shows. Bob Putnam said that 20 percent of the loss of social capital in America is attributable to the growth of television.[22] He actually models the numbers. Homogenization by television is probably a bigger influence than these other factors—gender, ethnicity, or generational differences.

The Story of the Brooklyn Bank and the PC Network

A long story but an interesting one on the differences in ethnic backgrounds is the tale of Brooklyn bank. In the late 1960s, I attended Columbia University for a while. Another guy and I were pretty scholarly. Columbia was up in flames. Anti-war troubles. We would hide together in libraries and we became very friendly. This guy rose to very high office in one of the big banks in New York.

About once a year, we have dinner together. One time, we were talking and he asked me, "What are you doing research on?"

I said, "Knowledge and organizations."

And he said to me, "You know, we have all the knowledge that we need. We just spent $84 million on a new PC network for the branches of the bank.

Now think about that statement: "We have all the knowledge that we need." Just by putting in place a machine in each branch?"

So I said: "You may have all the knowledge you need, and these machines may aid it, but I'll bet that's wrong."

We started discussing it and I said: "Why don't we find the answer? Let's try to prove it one way or the other."

So we made a bet. This guy is also from Brooklyn. He likes to bet. I said: "Let's go to a branch and find out why your branch performs so well versus other banks in the neighborhood, and see what role technology plays in a high performing branch."

He was responsible for branch banking, and he had a big map of New York City and the various branches were rated, "A" or "B" or "C" or "D" versus other banks. The fact is, banks sell the same stuff. If you're a branch bank, it's hard to differentiate yourself from other branch banks. You sell CDs and mortgages. You have ATM machines. There isn't a lot of difference. But the branches of banks perform very differently. So we found a branch, right in the middle of Brooklyn, that performed at the "A" level. It was a branch on a crossroads where there were three other competing banks. Why would this branch be doing so well?

So we said, "Let's visit this bank." We both dressed down a bit, and we drove to central Brooklyn. And we go in to visit this bank. This is a neighborhood that both of us knew as kids and we hadn't been there in a long while. And the neighborhood had shifted, as happens in large cities. It had changed from working class, Jewish, Italian, and Irish to two dominant groups. This neighborhood now comprised Hasidic Jews and Rastafarians. I don't know why they had chosen to live together, but there they were.

So we go into this branch bank, which is doing very well. And who's running it? It's Mr. Kim, a Korean. Only in New York! So my friend introduced himself to Mr. Kim. And of course, no one had ever seen an executive of the bank at this branch. This is no surprise. No one ever sees executives. You can work in a big company and never see the top executives. It's certainly true for most companies.

Mr. Kim almost fainted. My friend explained that this was an off-the-record visit. Mr. Kim was shocked, but we calmed him down and congratulated him. My friend said, "You've done a great job! You're an 'A' performer and you've won bonuses. And we're just here to learn why you do so well."

Mr. Kim was very nervous, and at first wouldn't talk much. But after a while, he told us what he did. He realized that what his branch offered wasn't very different from what any other bank offered. He said he wanted to understand his customers' attitudes to money and to disposable income and to work. He wanted to know what really mattered to them when they thought about money. They weren't rich people. What did they care about? Mortgages? College loans? Or what? So he learned the languages. He learned Creole and Yiddish. Now this is not an easy trick for anyone. He learned enough and he became friendly with people, and he'd go to the Bar Mitzvahs. He'd go to the social events of the Rastafarians. He got to know them. He was friendly, and he wanted to learn what they were like as people, as a culture. And he did it. He learned it. He'd go to their homes. He found that they bought brick homes. They didn't send their kids to college. They did this. They did that. They invested in short-term securities. And of course, he tailored the bank's offerings to respond to the way they felt about money. And of course, it made a difference.

He pointed to the bank across the street, the branch of another big New York bank, which was constantly stressing short term mortgages. Five and 10 year mortgages. "These people," he said, "have no interest in that whatsoever. They can't afford it. Don't they know that?" He was shocked. "If they'd just talk to these people, they'd find out they want 30 year mortgages."

You had to know the people to find this out. You could do market research, but it still wouldn't show you the nuances. It meant meeting and talking with them. And these are hard-working, working-class people, family people. Different attitudes perhaps, but good people.

So we were really impressed. And he also did something else. He was constantly in e-mail communication with the Korean branch managers of other banks. Korean-ness was a real tie. He'd talk to the other branch managers, even though they were competing banks. There was a very strong tie between them.

So finally I had to say, "What about the PC network?" After all, we had this bet. It was for a full dinner at any restaurant in New York for us and our spouses. No holds barred. No limitations. I had to make my friend pay.

Mr. Kim said, "Of course, we use the PC. We have to report to head-quarters. We get information. No question about it."

I asked more pointedly, "Does the PC network account for, or contribute to your understanding of, how you run this branch?"

He thought for a while. He was a very thoughtful guy. Finally he said, "Not at all."

So my wife and I were taken to dinner at Lutece, and we ate as much food and drank as much wine as we could in good conscience consume.

THE ATTRIBUTES OF STORY

We have talked about categories of stories. Now let's talk about the attributes of a story.

Endurance

One attribute is certainly *endurance*. Stories endure. Some of these stories change a bit, but they go on for hundreds or even thousands of years. Some stories in organizations endure a long time too. There are very durable stories.

I've heard tales of Tom Watson in IBM or Jack Welch in GE that constantly come back and back again. The endurance of stories is very interesting. The stories are the same. Sometimes the name changes.

Or the circumstances change. But the behavioral lessons are the same. This happens within organizations, to say nothing about culture and society. There, the endurance seems to be extraordinary. Stories about those wicked people across the river. There's a Nobel Prize–winning author, Ivo Andric,[23] who wrote a wonderful book called *The Bridge on the Drina*.[24] It talks about the stories that the Serbs and Croats and Montenegrists tell about each other. A wonderful rich novel. How enduring these stories really are, how rich, and how it forms the people who hear them. And it's true in organizations as well. The endurance of the story is very important.

Salience

Another characteristic is *salience*. How much punch does the story have? And what goes into the punch? I think what goes into salience is wit, and succinctness, and emotional power.

Three things make a story salient. It's funny. It's clever. It's moving.

Marshall McLuhan once said, "Anyone who thinks there's a big difference between entertainment and education knows nothing about either subject." I'm not sure that's entirely true, but it has some truth to it.

And there's wit: it helps if it's funny. And succinct. The story has to be short enough so that others can remember it. All of us know people who tell long-winded stories, shaggy dog stories. My wife has a cousin, a very nice woman, who tells stories that have no point. She's a very nice woman and you wait for the point. You wait and you wait but it never comes. They have no salience. They have no point. There's no emotional power.

> Marshall McLuhan said, "Anyone who thinks there's a big difference between entertainment and education knows nothing about either subject."

We respond to stories that have emotional power. "A guy did this one time in this organization and he was fired!" There's emotional power there. People think: "I'd better not do that or I'll be fired!" Or: "A person did this and got promoted." Then people think: "Well, maybe I should do that! That's the way to get promoted." These stories have emotional punch. And without that punch, they are less likely to be salient.

Sensemaking

> A story has to be true to one's own sense of how things work.

Another important aspect of stories is sensemaking, their capacity to explain. Does the story explain something and show how you should behave? Why did an event occur? Will something else occur in future?

There's the explanatory power of stories: "We did this project and this is what happened." It makes sense if it's logical and it's true to your own experience. If someone told me that he acted in a 100 percent altruistic way and spent all his time helping others, and that's how he got to be the CEO of a company, I would know that it wasn't true. It would not be true to my experience as to how organizations in America actually work. And no one would believe it. You could believe that someone was somewhat altruistic, but not totally altruistic all the time.

So a story has to be true to one's own sense of how things work. There's an "ought-ness" to stories, a prescriptive normative value. They mean: "Do this and that will occur." It's related to their salience.

Comfort Level

And the final point is comfort level. Are you comfortable with this story? Does this story not only ring true to your experience, but actually feel right? Even if it is a story about hate, or some wicked tale, does it feel right? Is it true to what you have experienced and does it reconfirm what you have already felt in similar situations?

These are attributes of stories that contribute to their spread, their endurance, their value, and how useful and important they are to an organization.

THE POWER OF STORIES

Stories that have these attributes play a big role in organizations, in fact a much bigger role than you'd expect from reading any textbook on organization or management. The importance of stories is not as widely recognized as it ought to be.

But enlightenment doesn't happen overnight. I mentioned earlier that I used to teach a course on Western Civilization and I'd tell students that the Renaissance arguably began somewhere around 1453, and they'd write down, "The Renaissance started in 1453," as though one day, on January 1, 1453, people said to each other, "Thank God, those Middle Ages are over!" Life isn't like that. You get these incremental shifts in different domains, and things move at different speeds. We have these great technology changes happening rapidly, but politically it's much slower. Social changes in organizations take place much more slowly. Some organizations are quick to adapt but eventually you'll see all firms valuing knowledge, the contribution of knowledge, the contribution of ideas and narratives, and the social contributions people make.

Larry Prusak: Reflections

AS KNOWLEDGE BECOMES MORE VALUABLE, SO DO STORIES

In 2001, I was talking about the value of narratives in organizations. In the 3 years since then, I've seen stories becoming more valuable, because, slowly but surely, knowledge is increasingly the source of wealth, especially in Western and Asian nations. And if knowledge is a source of wealth, rather than land, labor and capital, or more physical attributes, one of the ways knowledge is configured and transferred is through stories. And if that's the case, if knowledge really is the source of wealth, then stories become more valuable.

Firms are certainly beginning to value knowledge more. The process is slow and herky-jerky. And there are firms that will never get it, and they will just go down: their internal policies are still geared to a 19th-century model of industrial production, and they'll never get out of that. But the firms that succeed will be different, and they will value knowledge. If you value knowledge—really value it, not just talk about valuing it—then stories and their social contribution, the social context of stories, will also be elevated.

Microsoft is a good example; knowledge really is valued there, compared to some of the large hardware manufacturing firms. Microsoft really hires the brain and tries to promote the brain (as well as accomplishment). Most consultant firms, most advertising agencies, most firms where knowledge is clearly the input and the output, have to manage by knowledge. The smaller biotech firms, the genomic medicine firms, all of them are like this. Then there are "knowledge cousins" where most people are going to make their living in the future; for example, entertainment, style, design, persuasion, journalism—they're based on knowledge, but maybe they're a little different.

(I have big arguments with my own school district about what should be taught in schools. I think rhetoric is more important than computer science—far more important. Very few people make their living on computer science skills. But rhetoric—framing an argument, understanding the structure of narrative—I think that's one of the more important things you could learn. Law is 6 percent of the GNP, and what is law, but that? Or journalism, or writing, or entertainment.)

Some of the large manufacturing firms have caught on, like Toyota. It's become a great firm—a total "knowledge enterprise." Everything is about learning and knowledge and working together. Somehow, early on, they got the bug that it's important to have social technologies and to have a great respect for knowledge and learning. Let me give you a small example: A worker on the line, right on the factory floor, making the cars, can stop the line and type in a question that's flashed on a big screen so everyone can read it, and anyone with an answer can type in an answer or just go over to talk to the person. That's one of the great success stories of the world.

SOME STORIES ARE TOLD BY THE ARTIFACTS

There are also stories that are "told" by artifacts. A great example of this that wasn't there back in 2001 is Novartis, one of the world's biggest drug firms, in Basel, Switzerland. It is spending a huge amount of money ripping down their 19th-century industrial plant, which covers a great deal of Basel—20-odd buildings—and putting up a "knowledge campus" which is very, very different. This isn't just replacing one building with another, newer building; this is developing a *knowledge campus* to encourage knowledge transfer—watching how people work and developing spaces in such a way that they're more likely to meet and to talk. There's much more open space. This is a Swiss firm, and everyone was enclosed in separate offices, and labs were also closed off. At Novartis, they're putting in very strategic places Italian coffee houses, open spaces with marble tops and little chairs, serving expresso and biscotti. Very, very encouraging to come and sit down, have a cup of coffee, and talk to someone.

STORIES THAT TRANSFER SOCIAL KNOWLEDGE

Stories are one of the ways knowledge is transmitted, especially social knowledge. To pick some grand categories, first, you have epistemic knowledge, which is science. Science is codified, it's put into rules, it's written in articles (although a lot of it *is* transmitted through stories). And then you have purely tacit skills, such as swimming. But in between you have a ton of what I call social knowledge: making one's way in the world, in organizations, which is almost always transmitted by stories—legends, myths, tales, gossip, call it what you will.

Usually stories, whether in cultures or in organizations, are *transformation stories*. If someone tells you, "When this company did "A", "B" occurred and the output was "C", and "C" is different from "A", those are transformational stories, as old as humans, as old as the Iliad and the Odyssey, if not earlier. And those stories have a lot of resonance. Those are very powerful, whether individually or organizationally.

That's why I think staying in your house and working is just an incredibly bad idea. You never hear the stories; you never hear the subtext. There's a wonderful phrase that a Russian theorist used, not about this, but it's so applicable: It's the triumph of *content* over *context*. That's what depending on the computer is—just depending on e-mails and documents—it's the triumph of content over context. But without context you can't do much.

Let's say you get a job and you show up, and maybe you get an office. Maybe you get a cubicle. In some firms you don't see anyone: you just get a terminal. You have no idea how the firm works. I know a number of people who have recently gotten jobs at IBM—a firm I used to work at—and they don't have offices. They never see another person. Quite literally, they just have a terminal. And they have no idea what's going on. They'll never get anywhere. They'll never contribute that much to the firm, because they don't have a clue what's going on. They just get words on a screen, which is a very different matter than going somewhere, being and working with other people, and having a sense, through stories among other things, of how the work is done here, and how to succeed here, and what are the norms, and what behaviors are expected.

Certainly no one's loyal to their terminal. They're not going to die for it, or put out that extra effort. The Internet is sexy. It's fun. We all use it, but it's not where things really happen. The spark of innovation, where people get together and really try to think through a complex issue, that's not done on the Internet.

THE IMPORTANCE OF KNOWLEDGE

Originally, we were talking about knowledge management as a policy issue within firms. It's now become a huge issue, knowledge and learning; it's *the* issue for a firm—I can't imagine anything more important: how do we learn and where do we learn and in what form? *Information* is an article in a book or paper—it's frozen knowledge. *Knowledge* is what a person knows, an individual, or maybe what groups of people linked together know. It aggregates into the capability, the capacities of organizations.

I used to work as a consultant to firms in information management; those were the days when information was the big thing. It was the beginning of the computer revolution and all that. And I began to think—the one great insight of my life—that it wasn't information that made the difference. I noticed that when anyone had something interesting or important on their mind they wanted to talk to someone. They did not want information; they wanted a conversation. And I saw this over and over again. At that time, I was working in a research division of Ernst and Young with a guy named Tom Davenport, and we began to think that maybe it was *knowledge* that was more important—not so much information but context and rules and experience. It wasn't what could be codified in a memo. And so we began to write and talk about it, and it resonated with a number of people. Not everyone, but enough that it became a movement. And then sociologists and economists began writing about it.

Now there are seven schools giving a Ph.D. degree in knowledge management. A number of people started this movement, including three of the authors of this book, John Seely Brown, Steve Denning, and myself, each of us in different ways. None of us expected that this would happen, although looking back, the macro-economic forces ensured that it would happen. When you have an intellectual movement, which is tied to really large macro forces, it's not going to fail.

CHAPTER ENDNOTES

[1] Donald (Deirdre) McCloskey, Arjo Klamer, (1995) One Quarter of GDP is Persuasion (in Rhetoric and Economic Behavior) *The American Economic Review*, Vol. 85, No. 2.

[2] Don Cohen and Larry Prusak, *In Good Company: How Social Capital Makes Organizations Work* (Harvard Business School Press, Boston, 2001).

[3] E.g. *Building Trust in Business, Politics, Relationships, and Life*, by Robert C. Solomon, Fernando Flores, 2001, Oxford University Press. *Built on Trust: Gaining Competitive Advantage in Any Organization*, by Arthur R. Ciancutti, Thomas L., Steding, Arky, M.D. Ciancutti, Contemporary Books, 2000. *Congress and the Decline of Public Trust* by Joseph Cooper (Editor) 1999, Westview Press.

[4] Cornell University Press, 1990.

[5] Jerome Bruner, *Acts of Meaning* (Harvard BSP, Cambridge, 1990).

[6] Erving Goffman: *Behavior in Public Places: Notes on the Social Organization of Gatherings* (New York, Free Press of Glencoe, 1963).

[7] Harold Garfinkel: *Studies in Ethnomethodology* (Englewood Cliffs, NJ, Prentice Hall, 1967).

[8] Thousand Oaks: Sage Publications, 1995.

[9] John Seely Brown and Paul Duguid, *The Social Life of Information* (Harvard Business School Press, 2000); Larry Prusak, & Don Cohen: *In Good Company*. (Harvard Business School Press, Boston, 2001).

[10] William Shakespeare: *King Lear*, Act V, Scene 2.

> *Edgar.* Away, old man! give me thy hand! away!
>   King Lear hath lost, he and his daughter ta'en.
>   Give me thy hand! come on!
> *Gloucester.* No further, sir. A man may rot even here.
> *Edgar.* What, in ill thoughts again? Men must endure
>   Their going hence, even as their coming hither;
>   Ripeness is all. Come on.
> *Gloucester.* And that's true too.

[11] Hammurabi was the 6th and best-known king of the Amorite Dynasty of Babylon around 1792–1750 BC or earlier. Examples of his decisions were collected towards the end of his reign and inscribed on a diorite stela in the temple of Marduk.

[12] "By 1994, real hourly take-home pay for production and non-supervisory workers (who are 80 percent of the workforce) had declined by 10.4 percent from the post-war peak in 1972, but real gross output per capita was 53 percent higher in 1994 than in 1967... The public has watched corporate profits and executive compensation go up and their own wages stay the same." *The Working Life: The Promise and Betrayal of Modern Work*, Joanne B. Ciulla (Three Rivers Press, New York, 2000).

[13] *Marat-Sade*, by Peter Weiss. The Persecution and Assassination of Jean Paul Marat as Performed by the Inmates of the Asylum of Charenton Under the Direction of the Marquis de Sade. (Marat was a revolutionary assassinated by Charlotte Corday in 1793.)

[14] *Social Norms*, by Michael Hechter (Editor), Karl-Dieter Opp (Editor), Hardcover (New York, Russell Sage Foundation, 2001).

[15] Pascale, Richard: *The Art of Japanese Management* (New York, Warner Books, 1982).

[16] In the garbage-can theory of organizations, a firm is seen as a collection of choices looking for problems, issues and feelings looking for decision situations in which they might be aired, solutions looking for issues to which they might be the answer, and decision makers looking for work. Problems, solutions, participants, and choice opportunities flow in and out of a garbage can, and which problems get attached to which solutions is largely due to chance: Michael D. Cohen, James P. March, and Johan P. Olsen, "A Garbage Can Model of Organizational Choice," *Administrative Science Quarterly*, Vol. 17 (1972), pp. 125.

[17] Stephen Denning, *The Springboard: How Storytelling Ignites Action in Knowledge-Era Organizations* (Butterworth Heinemann, Boston, 2000). It discusses springboard stories, i.e. stories about the past that elicits from listeners stories about the future.

[18] Robert B. Putnam, *Bowling Alone: The Collapse and Revival of American Community* (New York, Simon & Schuster, 2000).

[19] E.g. Jerome Bruner, *Acts of Meaning* (Harvard University Press, Cambridge, 1990). Dan P. McAdams, *The Stories We Live By: Personal Myths and the Making of the Self* (Guilford Press, New York, 1993).

[20] (1) Cognitive science: Andy Clark: *Being There: Putting Brain, Body, and World Together Again* (Cambridge, MA, MIT Press, 1998); (2) The novel: Jerzy N. Kosinski: *Being There* (New York, Harcourt Brace Jovanich, 1971).

[21] See also the discussion of gender and ethnic differences in Steve Denning's *Reflections in 2004* below.

[22] Robert B. Putnam, *Bowling Alone: The Collapse and Revival of American Community* (New York, Simon & Schuster, 2000).

[23] Ivo Andric (1892–1975) was a writer of Serbo-Croatian novels and short stories who was awarded the Nobel Prize for Literature in 1961. Andric's literary career spanned some 60 years. Before World War II, he was known primarily for short stories set in his native Bosnia. Andric made his reputation as a novelist with the Bosnian trilogy (*The Bridge on the Drina*, *Bosnian Chronicle*, and *The Woman from Sarajevo*), which appeared practically simultaneously in 1945.

[24] Lovett F. Edwards, translator, Phoenix, reprinted 1984 by University of Chicago Press.

THREE

Narrative as a Knowledge Medium in Organizations

We do not see things as they are, we see them as we are.

—Talmudic saying

John Seely Brown's Original Presentation

In Chapter 2, Larry Prusak gave us a way of categorizing the different kinds of stories and narratives that occur in organizations, as well as their key attributes. His overview showed the many functions that narratives can play in organizations.

In this chapter, I will focus more closely on the barriers to getting change in organizations, and particularly on the role of narrative as a knowledge medium in various corporate settings. Once we understand what knowledge is, where knowledge resides, and how knowledge is communicated, we discover that narrative plays an unexpectedly large role.

This will set the stage for the next two chapters, in which we'll hear about some specific practical applications of narrative in organizations. In Chapter 4, Steve Denning will explain the use of narrative by a corporate change agent. In Chapter 5, Katalina Groh will illustrate the uses of narrative by an educational film-maker.

Capturing Knowledge without Killing It

Somewhat in the spirit of Larry Prusak, but perhaps less romantically, I want to throw out a set of idea sparkers or evocative objects to think with. I have always been interested in performance measurements, including how you measure things without destroying them and specifically how you capture knowledge without killing it.

There are a lot of ways to capture knowledge that kill it stone dead, and it's very hard to spread knowledge when it's dead. In fact, it's extremely easy to become over-zealous in trying to capture knowledge so that you crush it. Yet it's also possible to pay insufficient attention to capturing knowledge, so that you lose the value of it. To get the right balance between over-zealousness and insufficient attention, we need to understand what knowledge is, where it resides, and how it is communicated. It turns out that knowledge is partly tacit and it's social and it resides in practice. Practice provides the rails that knowledge travels on, and narrative is the vehicle that runs on those rails. That's why narrative plays an unexpectedly large role in all aspects of knowledge in an organization.

The Pace and Scale of Change Today

There is a shared context that we all have, whether we come from the corporate world, the consulting world, the institutional world, or the military world, and that is the accelerating pace of change. It's a period very much like 100 years ago. At the turn of the 20th century, electrification transformed the United States. It took about 20 or 30 years to catch on. But when it caught on, it happened very quickly, almost every aspect of how we live, how we work, how we learn, how we do commerce, how we build buildings, how we build factories, was transformed. If you look back at that period from 1900 to 1920, it was also the period when many new social institutions came into being. The boy scouts. Labor unions. ACLU. PTAs. It all happened in that 20-year period. It was a period in which everything was turned upside down.

> *Once again, we have to re-think how we work, how we learn, how we do commerce, how you build buildings, in effect how we live.*

We're in such a period now, a period in which computers and the Internet are permeating our society. This is a period in which the change is beginning to take off. It has nothing to do with dot-coms becoming dot-bombs or dot-toast, but something much more fundamental. Once again, we have to re-think how we work, how we learn, how we do commerce, how we build buildings, and in effect how we live.

The Ubiquitous Feeling of Fatigue

As I travel around and talk to people everywhere, I am struck by something else that we all seem to have in common. We all feel extremely fatigued. We all want the world to slow down. But it's not going to slow down. You might think of this as a period in which innovation reigns supreme. What we don't talk about much, and what leads to some of the fatigue that we feel, is the fact that during this period of basic change, we have to learn how to challenge and change some of our background assumptions, some of the stories, some of the deeply ingrained ways in which we see the world. One source of our fatigue may be that we are seeing the world slightly askew. We have to find ways to surface some of our assumptions and narratives, and reflect on them, often in communities and groups, in order to figure out how we can productively work with them and constructively challenge what everyone "knows" to be true.

Learning to Unlearn

It has become almost a commonplace to say that the key to survival in these turbulent times is learning to learn and to share knowledge. We say that sharing has to do with the exchange of stories. We say that learning has to do with constructing new stories and hearing stories in new ways. We know that we need to engage in agile experimentation and reflect on what we actually learn through stories.

But what hardly anybody talks about, and what is responsible for a lot of our fatigue, is not about learning how to learn. Lots of people can talk about that. A much bigger challenge is: how do we learn to *unlearn*?

Think about some of those stories that Larry Prusak referred to in the previous chapter, in Ireland, in the Middle East, and in Kosovo and so on. Think how they have distorted perceptions and kept progress from happening. Our organizations also have stories that have kept them from advancing as rapidly as they should.

So I want to reflect on the unusual and unpopular topic of how do we unlearn and on how incredibly difficult it is to unlearn what we "know."

Why is it so difficult to unlearn? The answer is simple. Every interesting piece of knowledge has two dimensions. It has the explicit dimension that we can talk about. But that explicit dimension also penetrates down into a dimension that we can't talk about very well, because it's embodied in us, in our practices, in our ways of thinking, in our ways of acting. We are largely unconscious of it. It has to do with the tacit dimension of knowledge. It's not a question of converting the tacit (the know-how type of knowledge) to the explicit in order to pass it on. For the explicit knowledge to be useful, it has to be deeply coupled with its use.

From this point of view, we might think that learning is something very simple. Learning has to do, not only with *learning about* something—we all know how to *learn about* something by reading books and so on—but also with, how do you *learn to be*? There's an immense difference between learning *about* and learning *to be*. It's discussed in the book that Larry Prusak mentioned in the previous chapter, *Being There*.[1]

How can you *be* a physicist? How can you *be* a doctor? How do you enculturate someone into the profession? There's a massive amount of tacit practices and sensibilities and lenses that we use to see and make sense of the world and act effectively in the world.

When it comes to unlearning, the problem is that we have to shed these largely unconscious practices and sensibilities and lenses. But how can we shed something we barely know that we have? We have this interpretive frame, constituted by our own mental lenses. We suspect that our current mental lenses aren't the lenses that we need for today's world, and we need something new to make sense of the world. Yet we can't even detect the presence of the existing lenses because we are already using them to see the world.

It's going to be interesting to see how far stories can facilitate unlearning. You can never talk someone rationally through a change in religion. You design or craft experiences. You go to the gut. That's what stories can do. They may be able to help us unlearn.

How Does a Motorcycle Turn?

The example that drove home to me the difficulty of unlearning came from riding a motorcycle. I have been a fanatic motorcyclist for many years. But about 10 years ago, I had to give up motorcycling, because it turned out that my reflexes had dropped about a hundred milliseconds, and a hundred milliseconds on a motorcycle usually means death. So my wife, Susan, and I decided that I should give this up. Then about 5 years ago, I learned that computers had arrived in motorcycling, and they had built a new generation of sophisticated computer-based brakes for motorcycles.

When I read this for the first time, I do all the calculations and I'm excited. I come running down the stairs to my wife, and I say, "Susan, you see, with these new brakes, I've just gotten back 250 milliseconds of reaction time. So while I've lost 100 milliseconds, the brakes have saved 250 milliseconds. I have a net 150 milliseconds! That's at least 10 years more to motorcycle!"

Now, it turns out that Susan isn't impressed. She isn't impressed at all. But she also realizes that she isn't going to win an argument about changing behavior, as opposed to merely exchanging information. So she says, "John, I'll make a pact with you. Go ahead and buy your new super-toy, but do me a favor. You've got to agree to go back and take a course in high-performance motorcycling."

"Susan, give me a break! I'm too busy. I've ridden cycles for 15 years."

"John!" she says in that special wifely tone of voice that will accept no denial.

I know what that tone of voice means.

I call up an instructor and say, "Look, I've ridden a motorcycle all my life, I can't believe that I have to do this, but I have this deal with my wife. So can I hire you just to certify that I know how to ride?"

He says, "Well, sure, you can hire me, and I can take you through all the tests. But I've still got to see you ride."

"Fine."

So one terrible Saturday morning, he comes over and I start taking the tests. Now one of the first tests involves showing that you know how to swerve. This turns out to be very important in high-performance cycling. One of the tests that you have to go through—it sounds brutal—is driving toward a 'brick wall.' The instructor stands just in front of the wall, and when you get to about 20 feet in front of the wall, he will signal left or right, and you have to swerve around the wall, and then come back within an alley of pylons that have been laid out behind the wall. No longer can you turn just by shifting your weight. You really have to drive that motorcycle, because you are going at a moderate speed. You know, you don't want to screw up. After all, you can't forget that brick wall!

Now it turns out that I am only going at 20 miles an hour or so; I'm just not getting it. I still can't learn how to swerve. I am making such bad progress that he takes me aside and says, "John, you know, I've just got to tell you, maybe we should re-think your even taking these tests at all. I'm sure you used to know how to ride, but right now, you can't do it worth a damn."

Ouch! Total crisis of confidence! My performance has now dropped almost to zero. We decide to go out to lunch. After lunch, I suggest that we try again. We go out and I persevere and eventually I do learn to swerve.

Here's what I learned. A bicycle has some of the same properties as a motorcycle. Bicycles are smaller and lighter. As a result, you are less aware of what you are doing on a bicycle than when you are on a motorcycle. Suppose you are on a motorcycle or a bicycle, and you want to turn left. Let me ask you: which handlebar do you pull toward you, in order to turn left? Left, yes? Well, it turns out that that is not correct. If you want to go left on a motorcycle or on a bicycle, you actually have to push the left-hand bar slightly away from you. In effect, you have to turn the wheel to the right in order to go left. You turn the opposite way from where you want to go.

Now that sounds counter-intuitive, but if you can ride a bicycle, this is what you actually do. On a bicycle, the touch is very light. But when you are on a motorcycle and you are driving toward this wall at a furious speed, and you are being told to push the handlebar as hard as you can away from you, you have to use a tremendous amount of force, so you have to be really committed to doing it.

This phenomenon is so profoundly counter-intuitive to almost everyone that I have tried to explain it to, I have ended up doing multiple experiments on bicycles—not motorcycles—to try to prove to people that it's true. What I find is that even after people have ridden the bicycle, and have actually turned right to go left, they *still* don't believe me.

So then I invented a tell-tale experiment, an experiment that couldn't lie. I took two ribbons, one ribbon hanging off the left-hand handlebar, and one ribbon hanging off the right-hand handlebar. The beautiful thing about a ribbon is that you can only pull it. You can't push it.

So now what you are doing is riding the bicycle holding these two ribbons and now you have to turn left. Which ribbon do you end up pulling? Well, you are going to have to pull the right ribbon. If you don't, if you keep pulling the left hand ribbon, you will keep going right. Actually, you will probably just fall over out of shock.

Here then is an experiment that brings the tacit to the explicit. Yet even when the participants can see it and experience it, they *still* refuse to believe it. I can go through the physics. I can state the equations. I can describe the experiment. I can tell you that it's true. I can get you to try it. I can show you books about it. But 90 percent of the people I tell this to just think I'm crazy.

That Strange Magnetic Force

Let me tell one final story for those of you who used to ride bicycles when you were a kid. This story works better on the East Coast of the United States than on the West Coast, where we don't have curbs. Did you ever, as a kid, try to see how close to a curb you could ride a bicycle without hitting the curb? I did. What happens is that you get within a certain distance, a threshold of maybe 3 or 4 inches, and then it feels as though a strange magnetic force is sucking you into the curb. You just can't seem to get away from that curb. You don't understand what that force is. As a young kid studying physics, this bothered me a great deal. Of course the reason is that in order to turn left, you actually have to turn right. Now when you turn right, the front wheel acts as a gyroscope, and the front wheel has an axis that acts as a pivot so that when you turn it slightly right, it knocks the bike over left. The front wheel goes right, the frame tilts, and this pulls the bike left. It's actually a succession of physical events.

> *I have drawn the audiences' attention to a piece of tacit knowledge that virtually everyone who listens to me already has, but even so, hardly anyone can accept it. Almost everyone is in denial.*

Maybe by this time, a few people I've told these stories to are beginning to believe me. But most don't.

Now just think. I have put multiple audiences through this experience. I have drawn their attention to a piece of tacit knowledge that virtually everyone who listens to me already has, but even so, hardly anyone can accept it. Almost everyone is in denial. Perhaps by now you will begin to believe that there is something possibly true about this story. And perhaps you will go out and try it. But if you try it, please try it in a safe place as you are apt to crash.

What can we do? Perhaps the only hope lies in narrative. Part of the power of stories and narrative derives from a story's ability to create a framework that our mind can understand. Through a story, you might at least begin to think about how to challenge and possibly change some of this knowledge that is tacit and beyond the realm of the conscious.

Tacit Knowledge as a Social Phenomenon

The motorcycle example shows how mysterious the tacit is and how difficult it is to get at it and change it. Even bringing it up to the surface so that you can do something about it is tough.

In recent years, we have begun to hear people speak about tacit knowledge in the individual, the skills that an individual has to do something or to be something. But these tacit components of knowledge don't live just *within* the individual. They also live *between* people, in communities of practice that are wired together in some way so as to create the organization. Stories reflect part of the explicit knowledge. But for those stories to lead to action they have strange tentacles down into the implicit and the tacit.

In fact participation is critical, and a lot of what we know is distributed across others. We can think about it in terms of communities of practice where people are engaged with others in a systematic way, sharing tasks and creating a joint practice over a long period of time.

Let me give you an example of this. If you share a task over a long period of time with a group of people, you learn to read each other in a very intimate, textured, nuanced way. The ability to read others actually starts to shape the way you talk and leads you to create almost a new dialect or language. Communities of practice evolve their own vocabularies and their own specialized ways of going about things. So this has to do with the tacit practices that lie in the group mind, as opposed to lying just in one individual mind.

For instance, take someone like Johann de Klerk, whom I have worked with for many years: all he has to do is grunt in a certain way, and I can already see a whiteboard filled with equations of what he's going to say next. You learn how to read people in your community of practice. That's part of the magic of being in one. The stories that we share with each other help to create some of the common ground for co-constructing our practice.

A community of practice is like a skilled basketball team where you read each other and each person is always in the other's periphery. When this person does something, you know how to react, even if it has just happened. You know how to read your own team faster than your opponents. The opposing team may be in a network of basketball players, but they are not part of your particular community of practice. You have to be able to read the moves of your own team and improvise and make up a strategy that leverages that capacity and also compensates for any weakness that might develop in an actual game. You get this very fluid continuing improvisation, against a background of being able to read the other members of your community. In true communities, you start to see special ways of talking and communicating.

The Tacit Knowledge of Organizations

This means that if we are to understand organizations, we have to pay a lot more attention to the social fabric underlying them. We have to focus not only on how *individuals* encode tacit knowledge in our bodies but also on how *organizations* also encode tacit knowledge. As we try to change organizational structures and processes and behaviors, we are actually trying to change the tacit knowledge as well as the explicit knowledge of the organization. The trouble with tacit knowledge of the organization is that, just as with the individual's tacit knowledge, it is almost impossible to get hold of it, reflect on it, and work with it.

This is a domain that business process re-engineering never knew existed. You could re-engineer a firm around things that had been explicitly identified as best practices without understanding how those are situated in a particular context. Many of the problems in business process re-engineering stemmed either from attempting to introduce processes that lacked an accompanying tacit dimension or from re-arranging the firm in ways that severed essential connections between the business processes and the work practices.

Descartes: I Think versus We Participate

Some of our misunderstandings about the nature of knowledge come from the traditional view of knowledge, which sees knowledge as propositional (knowledge *about* something) and has little to do with knowledge in being (knowing how to *do* or *be* something). In large part, this stems from the thinking of the 17th century French philosopher, René Descartes. Descartes' view of knowledge, in which all of us have been explicitly or implicitly trained, has dominated Western thinking and science and education for over 300 years. It rests on the belief that there is a clear separation between mind and body, and also on the view that all we have to focus on is the mind. This leads on to an equally clear separation between the thinkers and the doers, and eventually between managers and the workers.

Instead of Descartes' principle, "I think therefore I am," I have for many years preferred to look at things in terms of, "We participate and therefore we are." This perspective has its roots in various branches of knowledge, including psychoanalysis and the theory of narratives, among others. We come into existence, we come into being in the world, through participation with others. It is in participation with others that we come to a sense of self. Identity gets constructed from our relationships with others.

What this suggests is that understanding is basically socially constructed with others. It leads to a notion of knowledge that we can actually internalize and integrate into our conceptual framework. We know something when we have found a way to integrate it into our thinking and behavior, into our own conceptual frameworks and actions. That often happens in the process of discussing something with somebody, often through telling stories—an action in its own right.

In fact, a great deal of learning, even on campus, happens outside the classroom. Inside the classroom, you get information. Outside the classroom, you start to socially construct your own understanding. Most of what we know today has been learned by talking things over with other people or working together in shared problem solving. So we are constructing understanding all the time, in conversation or through narratives. We are personalizing it through telling stories, and in so doing we are constructing it for ourselves.

Abstraction, Generality, and Narrative

Descartes' focus on the individual mind and the propositional nature of knowledge led to a focus on abstractions. But it's important to recognize that what we know is not limited to the abstract. Indeed, Descartes' thinking led to the bizarre belief that the more abstract the knowledge, the better it is. Why would anyone think this? One idea behind it is that the more abstract the knowledge, the greater the chance that it will apply to more situations. So it's natural to think that if you really want to have powerful knowledge, it had better be abstract. In fact, the more abstract, the better. If you could ever render knowledge in a partial differential equation, you would be close to God. That's one point of view but a mistaken one.

Equating generality with abstraction is one of the most fundamental misunderstandings that we've inherited from 300 years of Cartesian belief. The generality of what we know is not the same as abstraction. It's true that an abstraction, if we can find a reliable one, can apply to many situations. But it's also true that there is another way to get at generality. One of the most powerful ways to have the general is to show how it is rooted in the particular and we do that through narrative.

What is a narrative? It's about building a powerful idea through the particulars. Every story has particulars. The way you construct a narrative is by joining these particulars—contextually situated, together into a moral, or the point of the story.

Those two elements—the context and the moral—enable you to apply the story to a new situation, and sometimes many new situations. So this is a fundamentally different way to get at generalities by using narratives to carry and situate the point. We often overlook narrative as an important practical way to get to the general, particularly in new situations where we don't have reliable abstractions.

ENVIRONMENTS THAT FOSTER PRODUCTIVE INQUIRY

Constructing Narratives for the Laws of Mechanics

Let me give you an example of how this plays out. It's a simulation machine built at MIT to give students an understanding of physics in their gut. These are the first, second, and third laws of Newtonian mechanics, like:

$$\text{Force} = \text{mass} \times \text{acceleration}$$

Some shocking test results led to the construction of the machine. It turned out that students who had gotten A's in their first year at MIT, who knew all the laws perfectly and could apply them on paper to all kinds of contexts, in fact had no gut understanding of those laws. They could not even sketch out what would happen if you dropped a bomb out of an aeroplane. They had the bomb going down straight down. These were A grade students at MIT! It turns out that the rest of us aren't much better and most of us also get it wrong.

So they set out to build a simulation engine. Unlike most corporate training, the idea was not to produce a perfect simulation. The idea was to build a simulation that helped the participants build a story. The idea was to get people engaged in constructing their own understandings.

So with this envisioning machine, the students would see the trajectory of a particle, and then they would be asked to mimic that by setting up the velocity and the acceleration of the particle at the initial stage and see whether they could get it to have the trajectory. In the process, the students began to have a feel for the relationships between the initial conditions and started to realize what it meant to have a positive velocity with negative acceleration. It was interesting to see these students glued to the machine, and even more interesting to listen to the stories they would construct around the trajectories.

We began to realize that the real purpose of these simulations was not to impart a perfect cognitive model of the laws of mechanics, but rather to foster a rooted, focused conversation around the machine. So we began to think of it the way that Katalina Groh thinks about her educational films: how do we create something that's evocative, but that helps the audience, the users, the participants, to construct their own stories around that?

Architect's Studios: Work in Progress Is Public

Let me give you another example of the social nature of learning. I spend a good share of my life in architect's studios, because my wife is an architect. What I find interesting about an architect's studio, especially those at schools, although it continues in the profession as well, is that the work in progress is always made public. I know of no other field where the work in progress is consistently rendered public.

In the sciences, you are often encouraged to think that it pays to keep things really quiet until the morning that your article is published in *Nature* magazine, and then you triumphantly reveal it and spring it on your astounded colleagues.

In an architect's studio it's the opposite. A context is being created by and with the architects working there. They can tell stories to each other. They are always looking over each other's shoulder. They are always drawing on each other's work and ideas, helping each other, and learning how to critique each other.

And when the master architect comes in to comment on something, learning is happening all over the place. Everyone is overhearing what is being said. At the same time, everyone knows the story of how that design came into existence. So everyone has the context to understand the comments that are being made. Everyone has understood the thinking that went into that particular object, even though it's been done by someone else. Everyone learns a great deal by eavesdropping, by linking and lurking on the periphery of other people's work. This is how apprenticeship learning actually happens. It's an illustration of designing for a "learning-scape," an environment that facilitates the development of these practices, these sensibilities that tell you what goes into really good design.

THE SOCIAL FABRIC OF AN ORGANIZATION

If you deconstruct the organization, you might think of it as comprising two components, one having to do with the authorized part of the organization, which includes the formal business processes and structures, and the other, which is the place where the work actually gets done, namely, the social fabric of the organization. This is where the social networks and communities of practice live, where the stories get created and told and retold, where the stories migrate, where rumors get created and spread. The formal processes can at best coordinate what goes on in the social fabric. But the real work gets done in the social fabric.

Information systems have always been preoccupied with supporting the authorized part of the organization. This is no surprise since any proposal for support usually has to go through a Chief Information Officer to get approved. As a result, a disproportionate amount of the information technology budget is spent on the authorized activities. In the past, until recently, there was little support for the social fabric *per se*. Now with the emergence of e-mail, the World Wide Web and intranets and instant messaging, there is an ability to build your own virtual community, your own communities of interest, your own web pages, and so on. So we are starting to see technology that supports the social fabric as well. Organizations need to look at how much they support the authorized part of the organization versus how much they spend on supporting the social part of the organization.

It's interesting to consider what we can do to help support the social fabric.

The Queue at the Copying Machine

Here's one that almost everybody overlooks; it has a lot to do with how you go about disseminating new technology. Most people don't think about it, but take, for example, the line of people standing in line to use a copier, a brand new copier. It turns out that as people queue up to use it, they become a support structure, so that those who are already in the know become teachers to people in the queue who don't know. Standing in line enables you to learn new tricks and pass on tricks you have already learned to others.

In fact, the whole notion of queuing turns out to be a very powerful learning mechanism. This really hit us when we put these machines on a network. We said to ourselves: "Wouldn't it be great if we could see from our desks whether or not the copier is busy, so that we would never go to the copier when someone else is using the machine?" The trouble was that there were never any lines, and since there were no lines, nobody was around to show how to use it.

Learning to Use Farecards in Washington, DC

Another example comes from the subway system in Washington, DC. When system was introduced, they needed to introduce electronic ticket dispensers. This was a new concept for the area. The problem was how to teach the travelers to acquire the tickets. They found that no matter how well that system was designed, people couldn't seem to figure it out from reading the instructions.

So what was done? For the first month or so, they placed 'experts' to sit by every one of the ticket machines. They were actually just kids who knew how to use the machines. These kids showed the people how to do it. Pretty soon, people began to understand how to do it, and they started spreading the knowledge to others standing in line day after day. It was a beautiful example of jumpstarting or bootstrapping the community mind. The investment was a small number of people for 1 month. It made all the difference as to how that technology got assimilated by commuters in the Washington, DC area.

Xerox: How Copiers Actually Get Repaired

Now let me talk about a more formal example that led to significant re-thinking inside Xerox about how we look at knowledge and knowledge sharing and knowledge capturing. This was also something that changed my life.

It continues the story that I told you about Paul, the expert troubleshooter out in Leesburg. The management at Xerox had asked me to figure out a better way to draw up job performance aids for our tech reps, some 25,000 people around the world who troubleshoot our equipment. "Oh, and by the way," they said, "could you also find a way to train these guys so that we don't spend $200 million a year sending them back to Leesburg for retraining."

I didn't consider this to be the most interesting assignment of life, but finally I said I'd take it on, but on one condition, namely, that they would let me attack the problem as I saw fit, even if it went against the corporate culture.

"Whatever you want, John," they said.

So I went back to see Paul in Leesburg, and said, "OK, we really want to take this on." Since I had gotten permission to do anything I wanted, I did something that was considered at the time rather weird. As it happens, I made, by accident, one of the smartest moves in my life. I said, "Why don't we try to understand how people really repair machines, not by asking them, but by becoming almost, 'them.'" By analogy, just think if we asked those people riding a bicycle to write a report on how they turned: think how inaccurate that would be.

So I hired some anthropologists. Julian Orr has become the most famous of them.[2] I asked him to go into the concrete jungles of New York City and Denver and elsewhere, and live, work play, drink, and whatever else, with these tech reps for 6 solid months and get the fine-grained texture of what really goes on there.

I said, "You can't ask management what goes on. They don't know anything. You can't ask the folks themselves, because they don't know what they know."

After that, Julian was to come back and tell me what he had learned, particularly about the tacitly held practices that the people actually used. And so through the engagement with these folks, we would have some idea of what these people were really doing, what their practices were, and how we might work with them.

> So after six months, Julian and his team came back. Julian walked into my office and said, "John, you're not going to be happy. Every paper you've ever written about trouble-shooting is just plain wrong."

So after 6 months, Julian came back. He walked into my office and said, "John, you're not going to be happy. Every paper you've ever written about troubleshooting is just plain wrong."

I asked why.

He said, "You've developed these beautiful fault isolation procedures, and you've built a sequence of logical troubleshooting scenarios but these guys just don't work that way."

"Well, OK, Julian, then how the hell do they work?"

Julian said: "Let me tell you how they work. What these guys do, especially when the going gets rough, and they have a machine that they can't quite figure out, they call their buddy, and together they participate in constructing a narrative that tries to explain this machine, and what makes it tick, what's gone wrong with it. How do they do that? It turns out that they literally walk around the machine and they start to weave a story. The story starts off trying to explain the obvious pieces of data, including the accounts of what's been tried. From that data, they are reminded of past experiences that they then use to generate a new fragment of the story, and so on. All the time, they walk around the machine, weaving this complex story, until finally they have a story that can explain every piece of data about that complex machine. When they have constructed this narrative, they have actually figured out the machine. Now they can fix the machine. And of course, if that doesn't fix it, then the story continues to evolve.

So troubleshooting wasn't driven solely by logic. It turned out to involve the construction of a narrative. But it's even more interesting what they do after this. Afterward, the tech reps get together in a bar or a coffee shop and they start telling stories and listening to each other's stories. In the social vetting process of telling and listening to and commenting on the stories, the stories get further refined, often becoming gems of wisdom.

So with those insights, we decided to use some incredibly complicated technology. We went out and we bought every tech rep a two-way radio. No computers. And these two-way radios were always on, so that every tech rep in that region or in that city was then in each other's periphery. Because they were a community of practice, they could read each other, so that they could tell when anyone was getting into trouble, and they could move seamlessly from the periphery to the center in their virtual world of two-way radio, and help each other out. So now we have an extremely good medium for telling stories and building stories by design.

By the way, this was also the way that we would do apprenticeship, because new people would come on and they could link to the conversations and listen at the periphery as this whole knowledge network was being constructed and pick up all kinds of new skills and confidence. And they knew that they could call on other people for help.

The biggest problem with getting the system going had to do with trust. Since this was a broadcast, even though it was a private channel, these guys were worried that the management would listen in. But when they found out that the management wasn't going to listen in, then they became very positive. They had open conversations. If you actually listened in on these channels, there was a seamless transition between the social and the technical in a way that would freak out some managers. So to make this whole thing happen, building up trust turned out to be critical.

XEROX'S EUREKA

So we realized that the expert system that Xerox had asked me to build wouldn't work. We set aside the artificial intelligence and the computerized expert systems. Obviously, we needed a community of practice. The challenge was that once a story was told, it would circulate in that city or region and be lodged in that community mind, but it wouldn't pass on to people in other parts of the world who had the same kinds of problems. This led us to design a system called *Eureka*, which involved thinking more carefully about how to build a knowledge base that we could actually ship around the entire world, to support the 25,000 tech reps in Xerox.

What Is Knowledge?

In the process, we had to grapple with the age-old question, what is knowledge? There have been many takes on this. Plato had suggested a couple of millennia ago that knowledge is true (whatever that means) justified or warranted belief.[3] That is to say, a lot of people have opinions, but it doesn't become knowledge until you are willing to act on it. You believe it enough when your actions are on the line and you are willing to act on it.

The new system worked like this. When one of these repairers had a titbit, a new idea or a new story, he would go to the system like going to the coffee shop or the beer hall. He would choose his peer review committee, and use the intranet to pull a peer group together and get the social vetting of the story. Once the story was vetted, it got lodged into the knowledge base, along with the name of the author. If the peer review group had added a lot to it, then the peer review group's name also went on this particular story, on this particular tip. What this led to was simultaneously building intellectual and social capital. After the fact this was obvious, but we were surprised by it at the time. It was building social capital because those people who contributed to this worldwide knowledge base had their names on it. And those who contributed really great stories soon became heroes in this relatively closed community of practice around the world.

These people had incredible stories. There were people in Brazil saving huge amounts of money by way of an idea that came out of Canada, and so the guy in Canada was now a hero in Brazil, and so on.

Their own identities also started to change. In effect, here was a system that simultaneously built social capital and intellectual capital. Soon personal identities started to be shaped and emerge through this community of practice. As a result, we not only captured intellectual and social capital, but this new hub became a platform for creating meaning in these guys' lives.

The Question of Incentives

Thus we had a triple win. Even so, we still had difficulty understanding the social dynamics of it. After we constructed the system, we saw all this happen. We saw that some of the ideas were worth a fortune, saving the company huge amounts of money. So we went back to the tech reps and suggested giving bonuses to people who were really contributing, and we asked for their advice on how to set up such a system.

And the technical communities themselves said: "No way!" In essence, they were saying: "We don't want extrinsic motivation to replace intrinsic motivation. As soon as you start giving us bonuses, we're going to game the system; it will undermine the system in terms of the social structure that we have built here." And so on.

Sometimes I wonder if we didn't offer large enough bonuses. If we had offered them a million dollars apiece, then who knows what would have happened. I think it would have actually torn up the social fabric that we had constructed. We would have lost the construction of meaning, the sense of identity of these people, the sense of being part of a larger community.

The Business Results of Eureka

What's also interesting is that we were able to measure some of the consequences of this by running controlled experiments in various countries. For example, we got a chance to measure what I call the learning curve of people in this community, using a 6-month controlled test, in a 2-year field deployment. They got a 300 percent improvement in the whole group's learning curve. To us, 10 percent reduction in service time and parts used was a huge amount of money. There were fewer long or broken calls. And customer satisfaction was up. The numbers showed that Eureka really worked from a business point of view.

OPEN SOURCE DEVELOPMENT

Another example is open source development. Linux was a consortium of individuals who built an operating system, thousands of people, using their own free time around the world.[4] They were led by a guy, Linus Torvalds, from Helsinki, Finland, and they created an operating system that is one of the dominant systems on servers. What's interesting is to go back and understand the social dynamic of the open source consortium. What you had was a small group of people at the center and a czar. And that czar determined what was going into that operating system and what wasn't. But the code was completely open. Anybody could pick up chunks of it. Anybody could improve it. You could map those improvements and send them back to the central czar. If he liked it, it would go into the operating system with your name attached to that code.

For the first time in my life, I saw computer scientists starting to write code that was meant to be read by others. Unless your colleagues could read the code, they couldn't pick it up and learn from it and modify it. So the open source consortium became a massive learning community, in terms of sharing of best practices by making code transparent, readable, changeable, and hence easy to experiment with.

So it was a learning community, but also a knowledge creation community. These kids would pick up code, modify it, see if it was better, pack it, and ship it back in. And if it made it back in, you became a hero. If it didn't, you tried some more.

This way of operating is going to become more important as we move into the 21st century. It entails a sense of engagement, not just narrative construction, but also what I call *bricolage*. *Bricolage* involves moving from worshipping the abstract to working with the concrete. Working with the concrete, in terms of a concrete piece of code. The algorithm may be abstract, but the code is concrete. And you take a chunk of code and you start tinkering with it. *Bricolage* has to do with tinkering—tinkering with a piece of concrete code and seeing whether you can make it better. You engage in *bricolage* until you have something that you think is better, and then you send it back into the debate. If it is accepted, you increase your social capital or reputation.

Xerox PARC

I have talked a lot about learning and knowledge captured in a very simple way. That's not the whole story. The more interesting question to me is: how do we stimulate radical innovation and generate radically new knowledge?

The Palo Alto Research Center (PARC) is a microcosm of a place that has fashioned an area for knowledge sharing and the construction of radical ideas. The best way to think about PARC, and about enterprises generally, is as a set of knowledge ecologies. In a place like PARC, we have multiple skills and multiple disciplines—everything from theoretical physics, mathematics, and engineering to ecology, sociology, and psychology. Now there are even artists.

It's an ecology of disciplines. Think about the knowledge ecology. As in any kind of ecology, it is a system. It has all kinds of dynamic interactive capacities. It has to be open. It has to be critically nurtured or husbanded rather than managed. You can't manage creativity. You can't manage invention. You can manage innovation because that's a matter of taking invention to market. But creativity has to be nurtured or husbanded. The challenge is to achieve a balance between structure and spontaneity. If everything happens spontaneously, you get all kinds of self-canceling behavior. There are too many ideas, and none of them is adequately pursued.

The question is: how do you put the backbones in there that enable and coordinate the creative practice without becoming stifling? How do you acknowledge both the structure and the spontaneity? How do you create a space for pluralism?

Creative Abrasion

Disciplines are not very good at interacting with each other. Just walk into any type of campus. The trouble with putting all the disciplines together is that if you try to call a formal meeting, a meeting of, say, engineers, psychologists, and anthropologists, it quickly degenerates into throwing metaphysical spitballs at each other. So the challenge is: how do you create a space of pluralism that somehow manages to foster and honor creative abrasion, so that you can get ideas that really rub against each other productively as opposed to destructively. You can use this notion as a way to challenge the status quo, to be able to think out of the box and to examine some tacitly held sensibilities, if not tacitly held practices.

> The trouble with putting all the disciplines together is that if you put different disciplines together, and you try to call a formal meeting, the meeting of, say, engineers, psychologists, and anthropologists, it quickly degenerates into throwing metaphysical spitballs at each other.

The Virgin Space

But to make this really work, you have to think about the shaping of space, the role of place. And for the source of inspiration, I went back to Peter Brook, the famous director of the Royal Shakespeare Company. This quote has shaped a lot of my thinking in the last couple of years.

> *"In order for something of quality to take place, an empty space has to be created. An empty space makes it possible for a new phenomenon to come to life, for anything that touches on content, meaning, expression, language, and music can exist only if the experience is fresh and new. However no fresh and new experience is possible if there isn't a pure, virgin space ready to receive it."*[5]

And in fact you need to take the idea of virgin space and architect it into the work-scape, so as to bring the physical, the social, and the informational spaces into creative tension and alignment. Because the challenge here is not just information. It's not just social. It's not just physical design. It's a question of how you bring these three things together in a way that it creates virgin space.

Wired Coffee Pots

Let me give you a couple of examples of some spaces that we've created to bring together people of different disciplines. These were people who in the formal spaces would just throw these metaphysical spitballs at each other. In these informal spaces they were able to have a conversation and share stories.

One of the things we did was to install *wired coffee pots* to the internet. This meant that any time that there was a fresh pot of coffee, a signal went up on the net. Anyone on that floor would know that a fresh pot of coffee was being brewed. They would come streaming out of their office doors from various parts of the building so that they could come and get a fresh pot of coffee. They would of course collide in front of the coffee pot. And so this signaling mechanism actually brought together people of different disciplines, because the coffee pot was usually in one area of the building, where one discipline would be camped out. This was a first step.

We didn't stop there. As a next step, we installed next to the coffee pot, *floor to ceiling white boards*, huge white boards, so that you actually map the conversation around the coffee pot. The context of the conversation could be made available to everyone, like work in progress in an architect's studio. It would lay out the whole context, the evolution of this conversation, and this would enable other people to walk by, look up from the periphery and see if they were interested, and, if they were interested, they could seamlessly join the conversation and be able to pick up the context of the conversation. That was *step number two*.

Once these conversations had been socially and physically jump-started, then *step number three* was to continue and build on them through time. We didn't want to tie up that physical space. Instead we wanted to find a way to get from the white board to the web. So we constructed *cameras in the ceiling* that would take 16 snapshots of this whole wall, and digitally stitch that together with an ultra-high-resolution image and put that up on the web. Then people could browse through that. They could zero in on any tiny part of it, and they could add to that white board if they wanted, and so on. It fostered the continuation of the conversation.

And then *the final step* is an experiment that is still in progress. We want to see if we can wire together the coffee pots in our place in San Francisco and in our offices in New York City. When we started, it seemed ridiculously expensive, but now it costs very little. We rented our own fiber-optic cable so that these two spaces are on the air, all the time, and everyone can participate, 7 × 24. We used this capability to hook up the commons area, not the conference rooms.

THRESHHOLDS, DOORWAYS, AND STAIRCASES

Here's a low-tech idea. Have you ever thought about the empty space that a doorway creates? A doorway is an amazingly safe place to start a conversation. If you don't like the conversation, you can pull back from the doorway. If you do like the conversation, you can invite the person in. In Peter Brook's words, this doorway is a virgin space. Think about the kinds of ideas, the kinds of conversations that are permitted, once you're standing in the doorway by stepping into that evocative space.

The Nickolodeon Building

Another example comes from Nickelodeon headquarters in New York City. At their headquarters, they built a center staircase in the middle of their various floors of this building. What's happened is that the staircase is used not only for informal social events but also for their company meetings. You see people sitting on the stairs. Dangling over the rails. It's very informal. It's easy to share stories. So the space has become a very interesting place. It's a space that brings different disciplines, people from different floors, and ties them together.

PRACTICE AND NARRATIVE

The Knowledge Paradox: Sticky, Leaky, and Intangible

There is something very else curious when you read the literature on knowledge management. There are articles that talk about how *sticky* knowledge is. If only HP knew what HP knew. They are saying that knowledge is created in one part of the organization, and it seems almost impossible to move it from research to engineering, from engineering to manufacturing, and so on.

And then, on the other hand, knowledge is also *leaky*. Take a place like the Palo Alto Research Center. Knowledge had a very hard time moving to Rochester, but it seamlessly slipped out to a little start-up called Apple, and to a second tiny start-up called Microsoft, and the rest is history. So some people talk about how leaky knowledge is. The same things that are sticky also appear to be leaky.

So here is something that is sticky and leaky and intangible, all at the same time. How can this be?

It comes back to that incredibly important thing called *trust*. It has to do with what communities of practice are so good at doing. When you share a practice, or when you have evolved a practice together, and you have learned to read each other, and know what each other is really good at, and because of that shared practice, there is a kind of trust and common ground that is built up, so that basically knowledge circulates amazingly well within a community of practice, but usually not beyond.

Practice: The Rails on Which Knowledge Flows

In effect, we think of practice as providing the rails on which knowledge can flow.

But there's a problem here: you've got knowledge flowing very readily in the community of practice over here and now you're trying to move it to another community of practice over there, where there is little or no shared practice. Why should knowledge, which flows on the rails of practice, move from here to there? You have a difficult time making that happen, because if you don't share a practice, it's hard to build up the trust and common ground that is required.

Let me give you an example. When we had invented a brilliant new printing technology in the research center, the chief engineer from Rochester came out to look at it. He walks in the door and he says "John, I'm here to kill this project." It's a great way to start a conversation.

What had happened was this. I had been thinking that this new technology was completely technology-ready, totally robust. I thought that I had all kinds of reasons to believe that. And this guy looks at me and he says, "John, when is the last time you ever delivered a billion dollar product?"

I said: "I've never delivered a product at all."

"Just what I thought! A goddamned researcher! Well, what do you know about manufacturing?"

"Well, I don't know much about manufacturing."

"Have you ever been in a manufacturing plant for more than a week?" I said, "No, I've always been in the research center."

It went on and on, and it turned out that our practices were so completely different that finally he said, "Now, you see, John, my practice is so different from your practice, how could I possibly believe you? You don't have the basis for making this statement that this technology is robust—at least not to me."

That was the beginning of a conversation that turned out to be very profitable. The conversation enabled the two of us from two distinct communities of practice to be brought together around a boundary object, which was, first, the technology, and second, a set of criteria used to move technology from research to manufacturing.

We could use the steps of the process—the set of criteria—to create a narrative that included the meaning of the critical parameters, the latitudes that would be involved, and so on. So around this boundary object, we could construct a new kind of narrative that enabled both of us to have some shared trust. It enabled the idea to flow from one community of practice to another.

Technological Support for Practice and Narrative

In the past, we have tended to focus on techniques and technology that support a relatively mechanistic view of the firm. Now, as we increasingly see the firm as network-based or community-based, we realize that we need to be building techniques and technology that support the knowledge ecologies of the firm, and eventually the knowledge ecologies of whole industries, knowledge ecologies that are full of people telling stories to each other.

If these ecologies are to be both vibrant and enduring, they must have both structure and spontaneity. The challenge is: how do we develop techniques and technologies that enable that? As we begin to understand somewhat better what's happening in the workplace, and replace our machine-based illusions with more realistic pictures of the richness of the actual situation, we may be able to develop and provide technology that will enable us to help each other, as communities of learners, as communities of knowledge workers that can share knowledge and exchange and create narratives.

Over thousands of years, we have learned the practice of sharing stories and creating narratives in face-to-face encounters. But if storytelling remains anchored in this face-to-face domain, it may be of limited value for geographically dispersed organizations. In effect, we may be missing the potential of technology to stretch the scope and scale of the benefits of practice, narrative, and storytelling. I know that many are skeptical whether we will be able to develop context-sensitive and supportive technology for the knowledge ecology. I am more optimistic. I believe that the real challenge in the technology arena is: how do we build technology that honors and supports the physical and the social, but looks at ways to augment it with the virtual, not replace it? And if we can do that, I think we have a chance to create a work-scape that would have more of a culture of learning and creativity.

The Lens of Practice

The key message for me is that we read the world itself, not through the lenses of knowledge, but through the lenses of practice. That is a very deep message, whose full implications I'm still thinking about.

There is an interesting balancing act between how you ensure that your *processes* provide enough, but not too much, structure—to be enabling but not coercive.

Obviously this is has to do with leadership that can create the spirit to have these processes strong but not over-specified, so that they become backbones for the ecology. A major challenge is getting the balance right at the particular moment in time.

This is why leadership is so important. Many medium-sized companies started out with excellent emergent practices along with a few processes to enable these practices to be coordinated. Then they encounter something that goes wrong and add a new step to the process. Seems reasonable, but pretty soon the process has become horribly complex and stifling. When this happens, the knowledge is simply killed.

And so the challenge is: how to use these boundary objects, around which negotiation and practice and the sharing of stories can happen as sources of creative abrasion.

In the past, creative abrasion has been discussed from a cognitive point of view. We need also to be seeing creative abrasion as a leadership tool that can bring different communities and persuade them to move forward collaboratively. This leadership need not necessarily be at the very top of the organization. People can lead from wherever they are seated.

John Seely Brown: Reflections

Knowledge Ecologies

In 2001, I talked about the need to build techniques and technology that support the knowledge ecologies of the firm, and eventually of whole industries. Since then, this has become increasingly central to current economic and political discussions. There was already much in the literature about industrial clusters. Yet most people fail to understand that industrial clusters like Silicon Valley are valuable in large part because they permit the cross-pollination of ideas. The difference between an *ecology* and a *cluster* is that the ecology reflects not only something that is organically living and growing but also the generation of innovation through the cross-fertilization of ideas. Part of the magical power of Xerox's Palo Alto Research Center (PARC) was that so many different disciplines were working in the same building that different sensibilities and different points of view could be involved in tackling some common problem. It resulted in the cross-pollination and remixing ideas so that there was an upward spiral of mutual learning that accelerated innovation.

The issue of off-shoring of jobs has become a central political issue in the United States. But what virtually no American writer or pundit or politician seems yet to understand, is that in certain parts of Asia, certain parts of India, Malaysia, Singapore, Hong Kong, and southern China, tight innovation ecologies that are specialized in particular kinds of skills are beginning to evolve. In India, there's software. In an area just outside Hong Kong, there's a capacity to extrude plastics and build great plastic moldings for consumer electronics. There are other examples all over southern China, Hong Kong, and India. These highly specialized ecologies are resulting in a radical deepening of skills of the individual and the firms in each area. These developments are analogous to what happened in Silicon Valley, which occurred first with innovation in the digital world of computers and software and now with biotechnology.

For all the current talk about outsourcing of jobs, it usually isn't recognized that this involves tapping into the deepening capabilities of these highly specialized ecologies. It's not just individual firms, or even sets of firms, but whole ecologies involving multiple networks with ever-deepening capabilities. So just as Xerox PARC works as an ecology inside the firm, and just as Silicon Valley works as an ecology beyond the boundaries of the individual firm, these ecologies that are emerging in Asia are having an impact way beyond their own countries. In effect, they are beginning to shape global economic development.

And this has suddenly gone from an obscure back-burner issue of sociological theory to something that is already shaping the political debate and posing a major challenge to the United States. It isn't simply an issue of wage arbitration, which everybody writes about, or passing regulations to "block the export of jobs." It's an issue of innovation: when ecologies emerge and bootstrapping techniques are unleashed, this can lead to a radical development of very specialized capabilities that change the competitive equation around the globe.

One of the keys to off-shoring and outsourcing is: how do you facilitate communication back and forth, between people who are sometimes separated by huge geographic distances? That brings us back to the discussion we had in 2001 on the importance of evocative objects, like conceptual prototypes that can bring together the different parts of the firm, or the different enterprises in an ecology, so as to create shared meaning as to what a project is all about. A conceptual prototype can function as an evocative object, much like a story does: it lets all the participants in their own way construct additional, nuanced meanings around the implications of the prototype *for themselves*. Simply sharing rigid design specifications doesn't get the job done. The key is to construct a context around a conceptual prototype, and then jointly construct understanding of what it is about and what it could be used for and what it could mean. So the intuition that we had back in 2001 around the power of the evocative object is likely to have an increasingly important role as we move to these new ways of constructing and executing projects, when the participants have a highly distributed set of specialized capabilities.

Indeed, the whole idea of rigid boundaries between different capabilities inside the firm or between firms is eroding, as people grasp the innovative potential of industrial ecologies, where there is creative abrasion and the social construction of joint understanding. Countries, regions, and companies that understand this will flourish: those that don't are in for a hard time.

The Use of Storyboards in Design

For example, take a novel information appliance. As a designer, it would be a mistake to try to define every aspect of the user interface and specify exactly how the user will use it. Instead what you need to do is to create a storyboard. And this storyboard works just as it does in the production of movies. People come together around a storyboard, and start to visualize what the project could mean for them in their separate contexts. In fact, one of the most interesting ways we did our best technology transfers at Xerox PARC was around both storyboards and video and filmed scenarios.

It worked like this. First, we would run a 3-minute video clip in which we would be the 'actors' and we would play out our preliminary understanding of how the new information appliance could be used. We would do that a couple of times. This would be for the corporate officers—the most senior executives of the company. It would give them some better understanding of what the device was for. Then we would say: "Now we want *you* to build a video script of what this would mean for you." And then we would use the storyboard to flesh that out. So it was the power of the narrative, broadly construed, first to bring the participants inside the story, and then to take it further, by saying: "Now it's your job to finish the story."

The first three video clips would be what I would call an *intuition pump*: this would get participants thinking in an imaginative narrative frame of mind, using the right side of their brains, and getting their intuitional juices flowing. Then we would push them further and say: "You're not just here to receive our insights; we want you now to engage with this. Please imagine how you personally would use the invention." And then they would finish the story. It was a process, first, of jump-starting their understanding, getting their intuitions flowing, and then saying, "OK, now you finish it and we'll work with you on finishing it, and help you construct the storyboard." This process functions as a platform for all kinds of inter-group communication. It's an activity grounded in narrative. It's the visual narrative first and then using storyboards to finish the story.

We found that this process based on narrative generated many valuable new ideas. It helped put conceptual meat on the bones of the evocative object. The conceptual prototype in videos with real people became an evocative object that would draw the participants in. The process becomes very powerful because it leads to the joint construction of the story endings, and it facilitates dialogue among people in distributed groups that are geographically dispersed. So this becomes a key element in making efficient off-shoring possible. The jointly constructed narrative enables people to leap geographic distances and cultural differences more easily. The importance of this is now much greater than it was 3 years ago.

Social Software

Since 2001, there have been major new developments in what you might call *social software*. The examples that I gave in 2001 were about e-mail, websites, intranets, and Eureka, which was the first major example of social software that helped tap into and support and define the "community mind" of 25,000 Xerox repair technicians spread out in a network around the world.

Since 2001, we've been seeing a whole set of new technologies being used to support the social fabric. The most obvious is *instant messaging*, which has moved from the personal arena into the world of knowledge work. Instant messaging enables people to have a presence amongst their small workgroup or their intimate community; they can communicate in an extraordinarily lightweight way, because in part they're always aware of each other's presence. That has a completely different social dynamic from e-mail. In fact, people on the East Coast of the United States tend to think of instant messaging incorrectly. They tend to think of it as 'Blackberries,' which are really just quick and agile e-mail systems: they don't create a sense of presence amongst the group using the technology. If you talk to a teenager today growing up digital, and you only use e-mail, she'll think you're a dinosaur because it doesn't really support the sense of extended presence.

We also have *SMSing*, or *texting*. Although this isn't particularly prevalent in the United States, it's very prevalent in Asia and Europe. Just as the United States thinks of itself as the leader of the Internet, so Europe thinks of itself as the leader in mobile communication, based on texting. And the social protocols of how you live in that world are interestingly different. For example, you almost never call somebody directly on their cell phone without first 'texting' them, because if you text them, you can find out if you're going to be interrupting them.

It's like knocking on a door before entering now in virtual space. That's just scratching the surface.

Then there are *blogs* or *weblogs*, in which people post an on-line journal of their thoughts and invite questions and comments. Blogs are a phenomenal way to support the social fabric inside an organization and to enhance awareness of what's going on.

And we also have *Wikis*. A Wiki is sort of a blog built for a community; it's like a community drawer rather than a personal drawer. And it has different rules for participation. It's no longer just a threaded discussion group; Wikis have the interesting feature that, if a viewer doesn't think something is said right, it's the viewer's job to re-say it correctly—the viewer can't just comment on it or criticize it. In fact, there are now attempts to build gigantic encyclopedias with Wikis.

And there are *friendsters*. These are devices that link together people who know people. We all know that everyone on the planet is in principle linked by "six degrees of separation" to everyone. With friendsters, people are saying: "How could we make it, say, two degrees of separation?" The idea is that if I want to find out something about another person, or get an introduction to them, I may have a close friend who knows that person, and therefore, I can get an introduction or a confirmation. Friendsters help map the degrees of separation in ways that facilitate connecting you to other people that you need to connect to.

Then beyond that, we have something called *RSS feeds*. An RSS feed is a way to have content streamed automatically to individuals for a particular purpose. So you can become your own aggregator. And the reason for this—one of the ways I use it—is to support the social fabric.

The University of Southern California

For example, here's what's happening in the University of Southern California, where I now work part-time. My job is to help bring together half a dozen different institutes spread out all over the campus, that don't talk much to each other. The point of my job is this: if these institutes could begin to have a shared vision, USC would be the world's leading place for digital media. Right now, the engineers don't talk to the social scientists. The social scientists don't talk to the cinema people. The cinema people don't talk to the communications people. And so on. There are silos of expertise, each one focused on its own aspect of digital culture, but they don't come together. They don't learn from each other. They innovate based on what's happening in their discipline, but not from other disciplines. Last week, when I was there, one of the younger researchers was saying something like: "Oh God, I wish I'd known about that talk; I really would have liked to have been there." And that's been the central dilemma in any organization: you either spend all your time trying to find out what's going on, or you sit in your silo not paying any attention to the rich resources all around you.

So we're resolving this dilemma with RSS feeds. We're finding ways to take feeds off the websites and calendars of all these different groups around campus, and transform the material into the format in which each viewer wants to see it. Then we consolidate the material into a running report, each day, on what people in a particular community of interest might want to pay attention to.

In one sense, this isn't new because even now you have people scraping stuff from this or that website and copying and pasting it or retyping it and so on. But that can be quite labor intensive, and many people just don't do it or can't keep up. What is new is that we're now able to use automated feeds that put agents on each website that say, "OK, now if this kind of thing comes up, push it over there."

And so we're now building a distributed awareness of everything going on around the campus as it pertains to digital media/culture. Almost no additional work is required of the participants, since each of these sites is already written in html or xml, and so people don't have to agree on how to describe things: we can put translators into the feed mechanism so that everyone gets the material in the format suitable to his or her needs. And so we're starting to knit together a new type of social fabric that cuts across these different interest groups, pulls it all together automatically, and repurposes it to make everyone aware in a very lightweight way of all things going on that day, or that week, or that month, related to digital media.

So there's a lot of new technology that has emerged with interesting consequences for facilitating social practices and connections in business. This isn't simply mapping business processes in a linear fashion. It reflects the complex and interactive nature of the social fabric.

BUSINESS PROCESSES THAT ARE ENABLING

There's also an effort under way to develop a deeper understanding of *business processes* and to move from *processes* that are basically *coercive* to processes that are in essence *enabling*. This concerns the design of processes that could actually help you get your job done and help you coordinate and connect with others, versus constantly trying to squeeze you more and more into doing something 'just this way' and pretending there are never going to be exceptions or that nothing is ever going to go wrong.

There are still people in companies who are trying to specify work processes so precisely that you'll never have to improvise and you'll never have to handle exceptional conditions. But the closer you look, in terms of doing ethnographies of what happens in any kind of work, the only thing to be expected is the unexpected—even in the most routine work. In the past, whenever there was an exceptional condition, there has been a tendency to add something on to the process so that the exception doesn't come up again. This continual patching process tends to turn the original process into something that becomes increasingly complicated and heavy-handed. Time and time again,

I see processes that start out one page long, and I go back 5 years later and I find that they have become 50 pages long. We need a better balance between structure and spontaneity.

So there's this sense of finding the right balance between letting people improvise versus trying to create processes that clamp down on them. One strength of the new social software is that it enables people to access information on demand and to improvise across a boundary much more easily than in the past. So understanding these distinctions between structure and spontaneity, between honoring our ability to improvise versus trying to eliminate the need ever to improvise, is becoming increasingly important, especially if there's joint understanding about the purpose of the activity.

Coordination and Narrative

Coordination still needs to be achieved, but often it can be achieved, not through procedures, but rather through a deeper understanding of the goals. And you get a deeper understanding of the goals, not by creating mission statements, but creating stories. So an important value of narrative, if it's developed right, is as a coordination mechanism for the corporation.

For example, take the coordination between research and engineering in bringing out a new product. Researchers design technology that the engineers will have to manufacture. How do you get a good hand-off? How do you agree on what the researchers should do versus what engineers should do? Let's assume that everybody is operating in good faith (which is not always the case, because one group may want to protect its own turf and make its own tasks less risky and easier). But for the moment, let's assume good faith. Let's assume everyone wants to get this product done in the best possible way. How do you make that happen?

If you have rules that specify that the researchers have to show the robustness of the technology up to a certain level, and the engineers are responsible for taking it the rest of the way, then each side tries to put on the other side as much work as possible. So the engineers keep raising and bar and saying that the technology has to be made more robust. And the researchers say that it's already robust enough.

The alternative is to adopt a different way of operating and build joint understanding of what's involved. If you can create a context of shared understanding, you'll hear the researcher suddenly say, "My God, I never realized it was so important to get this little piece built this way in order to make it dramatically easier to manufacture. I could change something on my side of the fence to make it a lot easier for you." And then you'll hear the engineer say "Oh, I didn't realize that meeting this requirement was so hard for you. We could compensate for that problem in this way." So what could have been a kind of a bitter clash of wills in the approach based on rules and procedures becomes something constructive and innovative—a generative dance—when there's a shared understanding. Suddenly the participants discover how they could do something slightly different that would really help the others. And so what would have been a contest now becomes a creative discussion, with creative abrasion. The result is that the participants end up with something in which the whole is better than the sum of the parts, having found the right set of tradeoffs. When they look at the authentic rough spots; they start to say: "Hey, maybe there's a little give and take here; by God if I do this, then you can do that easier." They do these micro-adjustments, and sometimes they even come up with a brand new way of doing the thing on both sides.

Now extend this kind of generative dance to a form of outsourcing and you begin to get the best of both worlds. We leverage specializations wherever they may be and couple them together into a process network with a continual set of negotiations, stemming from a shared understanding of the overall goal and supported by appropriate incentive policies.

THE EVOLUTION OF NARRATIVE

As to what the 2001 symposium meant for me personally, I'd say that it sparked a great deal of new thinking about the world of work and organizations. I have to confess that when I first heard about narrative and storytelling, I had a suspicion it might be bullshit. But Paul Duguid and I had just written a book called *The Social Life of Information*. And I had always been interested in how we under-value the social as opposed to the technical, although my background is computer science—highly technical. I have always been amazed at what we don't understand about the social. And I had also been personally involved in narrative: Katalina Groh and I had been working together on her films for almost 10 years. I was also loosely connected with the Cinema School at USC, so I had also been interested in the role of the narrative in films. I knew Larry Prusak. Then I ran into Steve Denning, and we said "Let's do this thing together." It was a chance for us all, from different parts of the culture, to get together. So that's why we did it.

Since the symposium in 2001, I've thought a great deal more about narrative and I've come to see the central role that it can play in achieving coordination. You can either force people into ruts to coordinate stuff, or you can pull them—it's either push or pull. If you pull them, you create things—narratives, evocative objects—that entice them to look at the world a certain way, and approach their work differently. I came to see that one of the most powerful ways to pull somebody is the power of the story. And it's not just the story as a thing, but it's how that story is received, and how it is co-constructed. What's so interesting about a story is it always gets re-purposed in the context in which it's told. The telling and listening to the story, both active processes, are always very situated. And the 'situatedness' of it is what creates the power. It's what enables everyone to see that situation, that context, differently. It enables a shared understanding through the joint construction of a story, and it thereby brings about an implicit form of coordination—which is a different and infinitely more efficient way to approach the issue.

CREATING NEW WAYS TO ORGANIZE

One of my continuing concerns, not just in this country, but as I run around the world, and particularly when I go into factories and companies, is that people don't look very happy. Everybody's being squeezed. Margins are being reduced. Deadlines are shorter. More has to be done with less. And so on. And I keep thinking: "Maybe there's another way to organize." In a sense, the power of the story, creating ways to jointly construct understanding, may be a way to avoid getting stuck in structure and to honor coordinated spontaneity.

Is there resistance to these ideas? Of course, there's resistance. That's because a narrative approach is challenging some of the basic assumptions of the dominant organizational culture, which is all about process and structure. Narrative is a counter-cultural thrust. That's why there's resistance and that's why it's so important.

Perhaps some other cultures are more receptive to a narrative approach, although it's difficult to generalize. Some of the Third World countries don't have the heavy legacy systems that we do. So sometimes they can start off in a more lightweight way, in which these ideas have a better chance of taking hold. And also, certain cultures inherently appreciate narrative more than we do nowadays (as opposed to not so long ago). In any event, there's something very interesting afoot here, and it's happening all around the planet. That's why we're trying to understand narrative and contextualize it and get it recognized as a worthwhile endeavor.

CHAPTER ENDNOTES

1 Andy Clark. *Being There: Putting Brain, Body, and World Together Again* (MIT Press, 1998).
2 Julian Orr. *Talking about Machines* (Cornell University Press, 1990).

3 Plato. *The Theaetetus of Plato*, trans. M.J. Levett (Hackett, Indianopolis, 1990).
4 Eric S. Raymond and Bob Young. *The Cathedral and the Bazaar: Musings on Linux and Open Source by an Accidental Revolutionary* (Cambridge, MA, O'Reilly, 2001).
5 Peter Brook. *The Empty Space* (London, MacGibbon & Kee, 1968, reprinted Simon & Schuster 1997).

FOUR
Using Narrative as a Tool for Change

*The surface of the earth is soft and impressible by the feet of men;
and so with the paths the mind travels. How worn and dusty then,
must be the highways of the world, how deep the ruts of tradition
and conformity.*

—Henry Thoreau[1]

Stephen Denning's Original Presentation

In Chapter 2, Larry Prusak gave us a way of categorizing organizational stories, and in Chapter 3 John Seely Brown showed how narrative is intimately linked with practice and all aspects of knowledge in an organization. In this chapter, I will talk about a specific application of storytelling to an increasingly common problem in organizations—how to spark transformational change.

At management conferences and in management books, we hear about all the wonderful opportunities and creativity and excitement and positive things that are possible today. But when we get to our offices on Monday morning, we often see a somewhat different scene of competition and distrust and difficulty, and we sometimes wonder whether these two worlds have anything to do with each other. This chapter is about how to cope with the office on Monday morning: what you do about the problems of real life in an organization.

The Problem of Change-resistant Organizations

The challenge that many of us have been facing is that in large organizations today, change is irresistible, but the organization often seems immovable. In the previous chapter, John Seely Brown pointed out that we are looking at a world that is going through a set of immense and wrenching transitions with an inevitable need in the organization to adjust to those changes. But when we go back into our organization and try to communicate the need to change, we often find that no one in the organization wants to hear that message. The organization seems to be immovable. No one in the organization wants to hear that everyone's working life is going to turned upside-down and inside-out. Change is irresistible, but the organization is immovable. What are we to do?

The dilemma is widespread. If you look at chief executives of major organizations who were hired to turn around major organizations and see how long they have lasted on the job, you'll find that it's often not too long. It used to be a couple of years before time ran out. But now you see it may be hardly more than a year.[2] A year to figure out what's wrong, decide what to do, persuade people to change and implement that and show results? How could anyone do this in just over a year? What happens is that leaders try explaining the change to the people in the organization and giving them reasons, but they quickly find that this doesn't work. So then managers often resort to saying to the people in the organization, "Well, you've got to do it, otherwise you're fired!" Or sometimes they might decide to fire them anyway and get a new set of people and start from scratch. But often they're fired before they can implement those plans. Basically, these are very costly and unproductive ways of trying to get organizations to change.

The methods are inherently adversarial and confrontational. They naturally provoke resistance and lead to many battles. Although the management may win some of those battles, it is hard to win the war. Sun Tzu wrote several thousand years ago that to win 100 victories in 100 battles is not the acme of skill. The acme of skill is to win the war without fighting any battles at all.[3]

Is there is way to get change in organizations that is more effective, more efficient, and more humane than any of the traditional ways *without* fighting any battles? Yes, there is such a way. It involves approaching things in a collaborative and non-adversarial manner. And the surprising thing is that it works, not only in the rarefied air of off-site conferences, but also in the sweat and difficulty of the real-world environment of downsizing and distrust and competition of the modern organization.

Unlearning What I Knew about Storytelling

I am going to tell you about a way of approaching change in organizations that is easy and natural and quick. As a matter of fact, I'm surprised to be telling you about it at all. That's because 5 years ago, when I stumbled upon this, I knew that knowledge was solid and objective and abstract and analytic. And I knew that something like storytelling was nebulous and ephemeral and subjective and unscientific. I knew that all of these qualities of knowledge—solid, objective, abstract, analytic—were the good qualities. And I knew that all of the qualities of storytelling—nebulous and ephemeral and subjective and unscientific—were very bad. Over the next couple of years, I learned how wrong I was. In effect, I had to unlearn a great deal of what I had thought I "knew" about organizations and storytelling.

THE WORLD BANK

The Starting Point for Change

I stumbled upon this in February 1996, when I was working for the World Bank, which is an international organization, headquartered in Washington, DC, aimed at reducing poverty in the world's poorest countries. It has been a lending organization for its entire life. It lends up to 30 billion dollars a year, and it is run on commercial lines.

It is also a notoriously change-resistant organization. Successive presidents had tried to change it and had failed. As a result of this track record, it had even come to be considered as one of the world's most change-resistant organizations—even the Mount Everest of change-resistant organizations. It really is a very difficult place to change.

In February 1996, when I started exploring the idea of introducing knowledge management in the World Bank where I was a manager, I could see that none of the essential elements were in place. There was no top management support for knowledge management. We had no mission statement. There was no knowledge strategy, or knowledge organization, or knowledge budget. There were no incentives for knowledge management. We had few communities of practice. No technology was in place. We had no tools for measurement. In fact we had none of the things that are needed to launch and implement an enterprise-wide knowledge management program.

These days, I sometimes ask business school classes: "If this is my situation back in February 1996, what are my chances of success? What are the probabilities of successfully launching knowledge management in a change-resistant organization like the World Bank?" They always answer either, "Zero," or, "Practically zero." And in a way they are right. From a strictly rationalist perspective, the situation was hopeless. But a strictly rationalist perspective is an inadequate way of understanding organizational realities.

Four years later in 2000, all of those things had been put in place in the World Bank. Management support. A mission statement, including knowledge sharing. A knowledge sharing strategy. A knowledge organization. A knowledge budget. Incentives for sharing knowledge. Over 100 communities of practice. The technology for sharing knowledge. A measurement system for tracking progress. All of the things that one needs to make knowledge management happen in a large organization had been implemented. The organization has been benchmarked several times as a world leader in knowledge management. So then people started asking me: how did this change happen in such a change-resistant organization? What meat were you feeding this beast?

How the Story Began

The story of the change begins in February 1996. Prior to this, I had been working in the World Bank for several decades and I had climbed up the managerial ladder. By February 1996, I was the director of the Africa Region. As the Africa Region was handling around one-third of the World Bank lending operations, I was beginning to think that this was a pretty important kind of position.

And then, as these things happen in large organizations, the scene changed. The President of the World Bank, Lew Preston, suddenly died. My boss, Kim Jaycox, abruptly retired. Someone else was appointed to my position. So things were not looking too bright for me in the World Bank. So I went to see the top management, and I asked them whether they had anything in mind for me. And they said, "Not really." But I pressed them further and finally they said: "Why don't you go and look into information?"

Now information in the World Bank in February 1996 had about the same status in the organization as the garage or the cafeteria. So this was not exactly a promotion that was being offered to me. In effect, I was being sent to Siberia. But I was interested in information and computers, and so I said: "OK, I'll go and look at information."

So I went around the World Bank and I looked at what was going on in the field of information. And I saw a scene that is familiar to anyone working in a large organization.

We were drowning in information. We were spending a great deal of money on it and getting very little in the way of benefits. It was very difficult to find anything. And we obviously had to fix this problem, and when we had fixed it, we would clearly save a lot of money.

But something else became clear to me as I thought about the situation. Even if we fixed the situation in information, we would be more efficient, but we would still be the same old-fashioned lending organization. And our future as a lending organization was in question. Many years ago, we had had a virtual monopoly in lending to the less developed countries. But now the scene had changed. Now private banks had emerged and they were lending far more to developing countries than the World Bank could ever lend. And they were doing it faster and cheaper and with less conditionality than the World Bank. There was even a worldwide campaign to close the World Bank down. There was a political slogan chanted by protesters, "Fifty years is enough!" So our future as a lending organization was in question. Simply becoming more efficient wasn't going to solve our problems.

Why Not Share Our Knowledge?

So I started to have a different thought. I asked myself: "Why don't we share our knowledge?" Over the previous 50 years, we had acquired immense expertise as to what worked and what didn't work in the field of development. We had a great deal of know-how on how to solve problems in agriculture, education, health, finance, banking and so on and make development happen in countries around the world.

But it was very hard to get access to the World Bank's expertise and know-how. If you were inside the organization and you knew somebody who had the expertise, and could talk to the person over lunch, you might be able to find out what the World Bank knew about a subject. But without that, you were in trouble. And if you were outside the organization, it was difficult to get access to the World Bank's expertise unless you were actually engaged in a lending operation. As a result, there were only a very few people around the world who were actually benefiting from the World Bank's immense expertise.

The Lending Organization

So I started to consider the possibility of the World Bank sharing its knowledge more widely. Technology was changing, and it was now becoming possible for the World Bank, if the management so chose, to share our knowledge with the whole world. I could see that if became a knowledge sharing organization, we could actually become a fairly exciting organization with a bright future. So I set about trying to persuade the World Bank to become a knowledge sharing organization.

I thought this was a promising idea. But when I tried to explain it to my colleagues, their reply was quite blunt. They said, "Steve, this is the World *BANK*! We are a lending organization. We always have been. Lending is what keeps the organization going. Lending is what pays your salary. Keep your eye on the ball! Knowledge might be interesting, but this is a *lending* organization."

Everyone *knew* that we were a bank. That's what we did. It was a self-evident truth. Everyone saw the organization through the lens of lending. I didn't realize it at the time, but in retrospect, I could see that these people had to unlearn what they knew. The brick wall that I was running into was the same brick wall that John Seely Brown talked about when he was trying to teach people to unlearn what they knew about riding a bicycle.

I could see that my initial efforts at persuasion weren't working. So I started to ask myself: how was I going to persuade this organization to change?

I thought about what the consultants did and I knew they used charts and slides with boxes and arrows. And so I tried using such slides people just looked dazed.

I tried rational arguments. But even though the World Bank is very cerebral, intellectual kind of organization, nobody was interested in listening.

The Zambia Story

And then I stumbled on to something else. I would be talking about the future of the World Bank, and how the future was going to be different. But how? What would the future look like. "Well," I would say, "the future is going to look like today. Let me tell you about something that happened just a few months ago."

We are still in early 1996, and I would say something like the following.

> *"In June 1995, a health worker in tiny town in Zambia logged on to the website for the Centers for Disease Control and Prevention in Atlanta, Georgia, and got the answer to a question on how to treat malaria. Now this was June 1995, not June 2015. This was not the capital of Zambia, but a tiny small village 600 kilometers away. And this was not a rich country: this was Zambia, one of the poorest countries in the world. But the most important part of this picture for us in the World Bank is this: that the World Bank isn't in the picture. We don't have our know-how organized in such a way that we could share our knowledge with the millions of people in the world who make decisions about poverty. But just imagine if we did. Just imagine if we got organized to share our knowledge in that way, just think what an organization we could become!"*

And that did start to resonate. It connected. First with staff. Then with managers. Then with senior managers. And in fact, it was only a few months later that some of those managers were able to get to the president of the organization. And in October 1996, at the Annual Meeting of the World Bank, in front of several hundred finance ministers, the president of the World Bank announced that we were going to do it. We were going to become a knowledge sharing organization, from top to bottom. We are going to become "the knowledge bank." It was official. Knowledge management was our strategy.

Well, that was not the end of the war. In fact, that was just the beginning of the war, because the people who had, just a few months previously, sent me to Siberia suddenly realized that the man from Siberia was back! And worse than that, he had somehow managed to co-opt a whole group of staff and managers and now even the president to pursue this strange vision of turning the World Bank into a knowledge organization. This wasn't just bad news. In fact, this was the worst-case scenario. So that's when they started using real bullets, instead of the rubber bullets they had been using up till then. Now there was a risk that knowledge management might actually happen.

In fact, over the next couple of years, there were major struggles, confrontations, and battles at the upper level of the organization as to what this thing called "knowledge management" was, and whether and how we were going to go about implementing it.

THE STRATEGIC DISCUSSION OF JANUARY 2000

One of those discussions occurred as recently as January 2000. By this time, we had been implementing the knowledge management program for several years. Everywhere there was evidence that knowledge management was a success. Only a year ago, the annual strategic forum had confirmed the central role of knowledge sharing in the organization's future. The mission statement now reflected knowledge sharing as a principal tenet. An external evaluation had verified the direction. A benchmarking exercise had selected the World Bank as a best practice organization. Internal surveys and focus groups also showed progress. Yet, just when all these strategic pieces seemed to be in place, just when we were getting credit for having everything set, all hell suddenly broke loose.

In December 1999, while on vacation, I learned by e-mail that some key senior managers, including some of the business unit leaders, apparently no longer understood knowledge management. During meetings over the past few weeks leading up to the annual strategic planning meeting, knowledge management had somehow become mysterious and even confusing to some of them. In particular, they were questioning the returns on the investment in knowledge management as uncertain. And these were the very people at the top of the organization who needed to be leading implementation.

According to the e-mail I had received, yet another meeting had not gone well. A routine briefing to the leadership about the agreed-on scenarios has ended in a debacle. What was presented as the mere fine-tuning of the knowledge game plan had led calls to throw out the whole program. In the heat of contentious budget discussions, the consensus that had been carefully woven together over the previous 3 years appeared to be unraveling.

On my return to Washington, DC from vacation in the new year, the worst was confirmed. What began as one senior manager's angst had now spread rapidly. At the upper levels of the organization, it was suddenly fashionable to attack knowledge management. One sharp question led to another. Criticism was spilling across the entire institution. The program was becoming the butt of cafeteria jokes and fodder for water-cooler gossip. Adverse opinion was spreading quickly but not in any visible form that can be dealt with simply.

In the hyperventilating environment, a calm, objective appraisal of the facts and figures was unlikely. We had had one-to-one meetings with some of the business leaders. We learned that the proximate cause for the disorder had been a series of presentations using jargon-laden black-and-white slides with lists of bulleted points and abstractions. These managers were not totally unaware of the evidence staring them in the face. But the issues lay not so much in what is visible, but rather in the mental spectacles through which these people were viewing the world. In their mind's eye, they could no longer see the path into the future.

As I had done in each of the crises that had arisen over the past few years during the implementation of knowledge management, I told a story. In the past year, the focus of our storytelling has been on the staff at large, without realizing that some of the senior leadership had lost the plot. Now we needed to re-target these people, the people who would have to lead the charge.

I have used the story of Madagascar on many occasions, and it has proved its capacity to move a group in many different settings. A new story would have been even better, but there was no time to find, craft, and test a new story for such a high-risk situation. In any event, for this group, the Madagascar story was still new.

It was a lunch-time presentation for the vice presidents and their deputies, with everyone munching on tuna sandwiches and drinking soda from bottles with plastic straws. I began only a brief introduction, and launched into my story as to why the World Bank needed to share its knowledge.

The Madagascar Story

Near the end of 1998, the team leader had a problem. He was heading a group of World Bank staff in Tananarive, the capital of the African island of Madagascar, in a comprehensive review of the country's public expenditures. The work was a collaborative effort with the government of Madagascar and a number of the other national and international partners.

The team leader found himself at the center of a mounting controversy over introducing a value-added tax in Madagascar. The purpose of the tax was to have a single tax replace other individual taxes that had become cumbersome to administer and ineffective in raising revenue, in order to ease the government's administrative burdens while safeguarding and enhancing public revenue. The controversy concerned whether medicines should be exempt from the value-added tax. Some favored making an exception in order to advance the cause of health care, particularly for the poor. Others were concerned about making any exception to across-the-board implementation, because once one exemption was allowed, others would follow, and the implementation of the tax would soon become even more complicated than the current patchwork of taxes it was replacing. The controversy was becoming steadily more heated.

The team leader was a seasoned professional with many years of experience in the field and had seen other schemes for simplifying public taxation founder because of such exemptions. He was therefore inclined to side with those arguing against the exemption, but as the controversy gathered momentum, he could also see that the debate could jeopardize the success of the entire public expenditure review.

What usually happened in past situations was that the team leader would try to persuade everyone of the wisdom of his viewpoint and, failing persuasion, would return to World Bank headquarters in Washington, DC to consult with colleagues and supervisors. He would eventually give the other participants the World Bank's "official position," in the hope that this would resolve the controversy. Often such "official positions" merely set off further controversy, which could last for months or even years, undermining the spirit of collaboration essential to public expenditure management.

In this instance, as a result of the knowledge management program underway at the World Bank, what actually happened was quite different. From Tananarive, the task team leader sent an e-mail to his colleague practitioners in tax administration inside and outside the World Bank—a community that had been built up over time to facilitate the sharing of knowledge. He urgently asked about the global experience on the granting of exemptions for medicine.

Within 72 hours, the responses came to Tananarive from various sources, including World Bank staff members in the Djakarta field office, the Moscow field office, the Middle East, the development research group, a retired World Bank staff member, and a tax expert at the University of Toronto. From these responses, the team leader could see that the weight of international experience favored granting an exemption for medicines. So he was able, within days, to go back to the other review participants, lay the international experience on the table, and so resolve the issue. As a result, an exception was granted for medicines, and the public expenditure review was completed collaboratively.

Knowledge management does not stop there. Now that the World Bank has realized that it has learned something about the design and implementation of a value-added tax, specifically how to approach exemptions, it can capture that experience, edit it for re-use, and place it in its knowledge base, so staff can get access to it through the Web. The vision is that this know-how can be made available externally through the Web, so that anyone can get answers to questions on which the World Bank has some explicit know-how and on myriad other subjects on which it has assembled some expertise.

And what's enabling this to happen is not just the technology that's weaving many people scattered around the world together in a seamless electronic web, but the fact that these people form a community. The fact that they know each other. Because when the task team leader in Madagascar asks for advice, essentially he's saying, 'I don't know. I don't know the answer to what might be a central question in my sector, and I am paid to know the answers to central questions in my sector. And I work in an organization that is downsizing and looking around for employees who don't know the answers to central questions in their sector.' And so he doesn't ask the question, unless he knows it's safe. And the only reason he knows it is safe is that the knows the recipients of the e-mail because they form a kind of community, and in this community, he knows that it is OK to ask questions and admit that you don't know, and people don't find fault with that. They don't say, 'You ask questions, so you're a problem: we want you out of the organization.' Instead, they try to help you find the answer.

The Impact of the Madagascar Story

That story enabled me to re-connect with those senior managers and communicate the idea of knowledge management. They started to think: "Well, that's remarkable how quickly we could respond to that kind of situation in that out-of-the-way part of the world. We need this capability all across the organization." And in effect, they said, "Let's do it! Let's become an agile knowledge sharing organization."

So the outcome of the meeting was not, as some had expected, my court martial or a court of inquiry looking into why there were so many flaws and blemishes in the implementation of knowledge management. Instead, the subsequent strategy meeting confirmed knowledge sharing as a key strategic pillar for the future. And so once again I found that storytelling was not ephemeral and nebulous and worthless, as I had thought in early 1996. Instead, it was a powerful tool to get major change in this large change-resistant organization.

THE FUNCTIONS OF STORIES

As I started looking into the functions that stories play in organizations, I saw that stories could be used for all sorts of things, including

- entertainment;
- conveying information;
- nurturing communities;
- promoting innovation;
- preserving organizations; but also
- changing organizations.

Different purposes require different kinds of stories, and it is the use of stories to *change organizations* that I want to focus on in this chapter. One of the most important things to keep in mind in using stories in organizations is to be clear on the purpose for which the story is being used. Because we human beings find stories such fascinating things, it is all too easy to get interested in the story for its own sake and lose sight of the purpose for which we set out to use the story. We are talking here about the pattern of story that is useful for communicating complex ideas and sparking change in behavior.

Stories That Change Organizations

How do stories that change organizations work? When I tell the Madagascar story, I say, "Let me tell you something that happened to our task team in Madagascar, and they got advice from someone working in Indonesia, and the Moscow office, and the professor in Toronto, and the retired staff member, and all this came back to Madagascar, and what we learned from the experience went into the knowledge base in Washington." When I say all that, the listeners are physically stationary, sitting in a chair in Washington, DC. But if they have been following the story, in their minds they have been whizzing around the world and back in about 15 seconds.

What we are looking at here is the phenomenon that Carl Jung pointed out, namely, that there are some parts of the human self that are not subject to the laws of time and space. And storytelling, the telling of, and the listening to, a simple story, is one of those things.

With a story, listeners get *inside* the idea. They *live* the idea. They *feel* the idea as much as if they were the task team there in Madagascar, not knowing what to do about some urgent but obscure question and then almost miraculously getting the answer so rapidly. They experience the story as if they had lived it themselves. In the process, the story, and the idea that resides inside it, can become theirs. It's quite unlike experiencing an abstract explanation of a complex concept. It's different from experiencing it as an external observer, standing back like a scientist in a white coat and appraising the experience, or like some kind of voyeur or as a critic, but rather as a participant, someone who is actually living and experiencing and feeling the story.

What the Story Explains

What is it that is being explained by the story? As we all know by now, knowledge management is a complex idea. I don't know whether it has 10 dimensions, or 20 dimensions, but it's certainly got lots of dimensions that need to be mastered if it is going to be implemented successfully across a large organization. Let's say for the sake of argument that knowledge management has 16 dimensions.[4]

If I say to an audience, "Let me explain to you in detail and depth right now each and every one of the 16 dimensions of knowledge management," I find that the audience is already looking at their watches and thinking, "How do I get out of this meeting without causing a big incident?" No one looks forward to a comprehensive explanation of knowledge management's 16 dimensions.

If I say to the audience, "Let me show you a chart," they usually look dazed.

Many people ask me: "Why doesn't a chart work? Surely a picture is worth a thousand words?" My reply is that we need to think about what a picture can and cannot do. In particular, we need to consider whether it is even theoretically possible that a chart could convey a complicated idea like knowledge management with perhaps 16 dimensions. The underlying problem is that depicting a 16-dimensional idea is very difficult, if not impossible, to do in a drawing. Two, or 3, or 4 dimensions can be depicted in a drawing, but with 16 dimensions, one really needs to be a professional mathematician to be able to grasp it.

But if I say to an audience, "Let me tell you what happened in Zambia just a few months ago," that is to say, a story, the immediate reaction of the audience is, "Yes, I'd like to hear about it." They're not sure what story I'm going to throw at them, but they've heard so many interesting stories in their lives, they have a positive attitude and expectation to the prospect of hearing a new story. I may lose their interest if I tell them a boring story, or if I tell an interesting story poorly, but their initial attitude and expectation toward hearing a story is positive. So if I offer to tell a story, then I start out, unlike an abstract explanation or the chart, with some initial interest on the part of the listeners.

Some of you may be asking yourselves, "How could this possibly work? How could a 29 word story like the Zambia story possibly convey to an audience a 16-dimensional concept like knowledge management? That's one dimension for every two words. How is that possible?"

The reality is that if you adopt the traditional view of communications, it's not possible. The traditional view of communications runs something like this:

> *I am talking to an audience. So my head must be full of stuff. The audience is sitting there more or less silent, apparently listening, so their heads must essentially be empty. And the object of my communication is to download the stuff that is in my full brain into their empty heads.*

In other words, communication is some kind of computer download. It's not too far removed from what Larry Prusak called the Monty Python theory of learning, in which the listeners' heads are split open and "knowledge" is poured into it.

There are many things wrong with this picture, and, overall, it is total nonsense. It's not simply that I don't happen to have all the answers about the 16 dimensions of knowledge management to give to the audience. And even if I did, I couldn't transmit them to the audience in the time that they have available. More fundamentally, the flaw is that that the audience's heads are not empty. Their heads are full of understanding about how the world works, where Zambia is, what malaria is, what the World Wide Web is, and so on. All of those things are there in their minds. And all I need is a tiny fuse of a story that can link up with all of this tacit understanding that they have in their minds. If I can succeed in igniting that understanding, then suddenly a new pattern of understanding can flash into their minds, and they can see at once how the world fits together in quite a different way from what they had previously been thinking.

The Little Voice in the Head

For each member of the audience, there are actually two listeners. When I look at the audience, I see the physical person in front of me, but there is also a second listener who is known as "the little voice in the head." We all know what the little voice in the head is. And if you're asking yourself, "What is Steve talking about? What on earth does he mean by 'the little voice in the head?'" Well, that's exactly the little voice that I mean!

It's extraordinary how little has been written on the phenomenon of inward speech, this discourse that we conduct incessantly with ourselves. George Steiner points out that it remains largely *terra incognita* in linguistics, in poetics, in epistemology, even though this unvoiced soliloquy far exceeds in volume language used for outward communication.[5]

But incessant it is. So for every physical person in the audience, there are not one but two listeners. I may be talking to the audience about Zambia. But the little voice in the head of the listener may well be saying, "I've got all these problems back in my office, my in-box is filling up, I've got e-mail to answer. How can I slip out of here!" So the little voice may not be listening at all to what I am talking about and may be distracting the listener from paying any real attention to what I am saying.

The conventional view of communications is simply to ignore the little voice in the head. The approach is to hope that the little voice stays quiet and that my message will somehow get through. Unfortunately, the little voice in the head often *doesn't stay quiet*. Often, the little voice in the head gets busy, and before the speaker knows it, or even guesses it, the listener is getting a whole new—and often unwelcome—perspective on what the speaker is talking about.

So I am suggesting something different. I am saying: don't *ignore* the little voice in the head. Instead *work with* it. *Engage* it. And the way that you engage the little voice in the head is to give it something to do. You tell a story in a way that elicits a second story from the little voice in the head.

And so when I say to the audience, "Let me tell you about something that happened in Zambia, I am hoping that the little voice in the head is saying, "We're working in highways. Why couldn't we do this in highways?" Or if you are working in finance, "Why don't we do this in finance?" Or if you are working in Asia, "Why don't we try this in Asia?" In effect, the little voice starts to imagine a new story, a new set of actions for the listener, a new future. And if things are going well, the little voice in the head starts to flesh out the picture. It starts to say: "Of course, we would have to have a community. And we would need to get organized. And we would need budgets to make it happen. And we would have to get more people involved. So why don't we do it? Why don't we get on with making this happen?"

And when this phenomenon occurs, the little voice is already racing ahead to figure out how to implement the change idea in the organization. And because the listeners have created the idea, they like it. They created the idea. It's their own wonderful idea!

The Knowing–Doing Gap

There's a lot of talk these days about closing the knowing-doing gap, and a best-selling book has been written about it.[6] People know what to do, but they don't do it! It's a big problem in organizations today. Well, I'm talking, not so much about *closing* the knowing-doing gap, as *eliminating* the knowing-doing gap. How could this be?

If I say to people, "I want you to launch tomorrow morning a knowledge-sharing program in your unit with the following 16 dimensions," then this idea, *my* idea, is coming at the listeners like a missile. It's *a strange, foreign idea,* and it's entering *their* territory, and they are starting to think, "How can I somehow deal with this incoming missile? How can I get out of its path?" And so here we are, right in the middle of the knowing-doing gap.

But if I say, "Let me tell you about something that happened in Madagascar just a little while ago," then something different happens. Then the listener may start to imagine, "Well, if that's how it worked in Madagascar, which was pretty neat, maybe we could start to do the same thing in my unit." And so the little voice is starting to make the idea the listener's idea. And of course, we all love our own ideas. And the little voice is starting to think through implementation, even while the speaker is still speaking. So there is no knowing-doing gap. There is nothing to get in the way of implementing the idea.

Telling the Same Story

When you tell a story that resonates with the listener, you find that people start to tell the same story. In the Fall of 1998, shortly after I told a story about knowledge sharing in the context of Pakistan highways to the president of the World Bank,[7] I was in a meeting, about a month later, a very large meeting in the World Bank, with several hundred people, lots of outsiders, a big high-profile occasion, and someone else told the same story—the Pakistan highways story. And as it happened, the president of the World Bank was there, and the presenter made his presentation and in the course of it, told the Pakistan story. And immediately after the presentation was over, the president of the World Bank intervened and said, "Well, you told the Pakistan highways story, but you didn't tell it in the right way. Let me tell you the Pakistan highway story the way it is meant to be told." And he proceeded to tell the Pakistan story the way he thought it should be told. And he told it very well. He told with verve, with flair, and with passion.

This happened in part because that story, the Pakistan highways story, which he had heard a month previously, had become part of him.

It had become a lens through which he saw the world, himself, and the organization of which he was president. It had become part of his very sense of identity, and his sense of the organization's identity. So for someone to tell the story in a way that was different from the way that he had understood it was to create a view of the world that was at odds with his. The only way to remove the distortion and make his world look right again was to re-tell the story in the way it should be told. He couldn't let the situation go by without intervening and remedying the distortion of perspective that telling the story in a different way had created.

This phenomenon is captured in this wonderful Brazilian proverb: "When we dream alone, it's just a dream. But when we dream together, it is the beginning of a new reality."

So we are talking about launching a process of collective dreaming together, with a group of people imagining what the world *could* be like. And if you can get that process going, and if the audience has the power to realize the dream, then before you know it, the dream starts to become a reality.

We often imagine that practical reality of large organizations is hard and intractable and difficult to change. What we don't always realize is that ideas can be more powerful than this apparently hard intractable reality. If we can get the ideas going in the right way, the existing reality succumbs to it and the dream becomes the new reality.

What Are the Limitations?

What are the limitations to using a story to spark change? We thought: if one story is good, many stories must be even better. So we recruited a couple of people, and they put together 25 wonderful stories, and we put them in a booklet and put them in newsletters and distributed them all over the organization. What was the result? As far as we could see, they had absolutely no impact. No excitement. No interest. No sign of any new activity. No discernible impact on the organization at all.

So then we said, "Well, fine, so print doesn't work. How about video? Surely video will work. Let's try video." And so we put together a video that told these same stories that had been so effective in oral presentations. And the truth is that most of those videos ended up sitting on the shelf in my office in the World Bank. They also had no discernible impact in the organization.

What we discovered was that there is huge divide between the things that are visible and discernible in the organization, that is, the facts, the actions, the policies, the processes, the things that are invisible and intangible—the values, the attitudes, the narratives, the life narratives, the underlying assumptions. We spend most of our time in organizations talking and thinking about the visible and discernible things, the facts, and the actions and the processes, even though it is the invisible values and attitudes and narratives that are actually driving most of what is going on.

In effect, when we issued those booklets and videos we didn't get to realm of values and attitudes and narratives. The booklets and videos simply became part of the visible and discernible things in the organization. They became additional artifacts. They were simply more of the stuff that is lying around in any organization in huge quantities. They never entered the invisible realm of values and attitudes and narratives that are driving an organization.

In the written word, there is often a disconnect between the speaker and the spoken. Often the reader is not quite sure who is saying the words. So the words tend to lack authenticity. In many organizations, lack of authenticity is a huge problem for the management. When the managers issue a written statement, the readers often have little sense of genuineness or integrity in what is written, and little confidence that even the author of the words believes what is written. The words are a mere blur spewed forth by "the system."

But if I am telling you a story, face to face, eyeball to eyeball, it's me and you interacting: then something quite different is going on. The listeners can see me and feel me and listen to me and can tell if I really mean what I am saying. They may or may not end up believing me, but at least they can tell if it's authentic. And so we found that it was oral storytelling that in fact had the large impact, not putting stories into booklets and videos. We discovered that it wasn't *story* that was having the impact, but *storytelling*.

This doesn't mean that you can't achieve big effects with books and videos, but they work in different kinds of ways. At the Smithsonian symposium in April 2001, we showed some videos of real lives, told in a different way, and they had a large impact.[8]

And of course, lengthy written stories like novels have always communicated stories in their own way, often very powerfully. A book may take 8 hours or longer to read. But in an organizational setting, you don't have 8 hours of the listener's time. You may have no more than minutes, or even seconds, to get your point across. In this context, a book is too slow, whereas an oral story can get the job done in that short timeframe. So it's not that videos and books don't work. It's just that they work in different kinds of ways from oral story-telling.

Do All Stories Work This Way?

Do all stories work this way? No, they don't. The stories that worked for us to spring the listeners to a new level of understanding had a very similar pattern.

The stories had to be *understandable* to the audience that hears them. If the audience hears the Madagascar story, they have to know that there is a country called Madagascar. They have to know that there are tax systems with certain kind of issues. They have to know e-mail exists and so on. They have to know these things to understand the story.

And the story needs to be *told from the perspective of a single protagonist*, a single individual who is in a situation that is typical of that organization. For us in the World Bank, the typical predicament is someone in operations who is in an out-of-the-way part of the world and desperately needs the answer to a problem. If it is an oil company, it would be an oil driller. If it is a sales organization, it would be a salesman. Someone whom everyone in that organization can instantly understand, empathize with, resonate with their dilemma, and understand what that person is going through.

The story needs to have a certain *strangeness* or *incongruity*. It needs to be somewhat odd but also *plausible*. "That's remarkable that you could get an answer to a question like that in such a short timeframe—within 48 hours, even though you're in Madagascar. But it's plausible. It could have happened. The tax administration community exists. E-mail exists. The Web exists. Yes, indeed, this could have happened in the way that the story is being told."

And the story needs to *embody the change idea as fully as possible*. If the listeners have followed the Madagascar story, they have experienced the main elements of knowledge sharing in the World Bank. They have experienced the full gamut of the idea.

The story should be as *recent as possible*. "This happened last week" conveys a sense of urgency. Older stories can also work, but fresh is better.

The Story Must Be True

And in my experience, it is essential that the story be based on a true story. When *The New York Times* wrote an article about my book, *The Springboard*, their headline was: "Storytelling only works if the tale is true." And I agree with this. The truth of the story is a key part of getting the springboard effect. It's the truth of the story that helps give it salience. If, by contrast, I tell a fictional story about what might happen if we were to implement knowledge management, the reaction tends to be: "That will never happen around here!" But when the story has actually happened not long ago to one of our task teams, then the listeners have to deal with this. They have to reckon with something that has actually happened. So I agree with *The New York Times*, the truth of the story is crucial. It's the same thing you heard from your mother. "Do not tell a lie!" It's not a good idea to go round saying things that aren't true.

The Story Is Told in a Minimalist Fashion

The story also needs to be told as simply as possible. In other words, I don't use the standard tricks of an entertainment storyteller. In the Zambia story, I talk about "a health worker in Zambia." I don't tell the audience whether the health worker in Zambia was a man or a woman. I don't tell them whether it was a doctor or a nurse. I don't give them the color of the hair or the eyes. I don't tell them whether it was hot or cold, quiet or noisy. I don't tell them whether the air was fresh or dusty. All of the tricks that would embed the audience in the granular reality of the situation in Zambia, I set aside. All of the things that get involved in the situation of that health worker in Zambia, I set aside, because I have a different objective. I don't want them too interested in Zambia. My objective is to create a space for the little voice in the head to tell a new story, that is, to generate a new narrative based on the listener's context and drawing on the listener's intelligence. If I get the audience too interested in the situation in Zambia, they may never get around to inventing their own stories. The kind of story is thus quite different from telling a story for entertainment purposes. I give them just enough detail to follow the story, but not enough to get them thinking too much about the details of the explicit story. So I tell the story in a very minimalist fashion.

The Story Must Have a Happy Ending

Finally, Hollywood is right. For a story to spark action, it must have a happy ending. I have had no success in telling a story: "Let me tell you about an organization that didn't implement knowledge management and it went bankrupt." The story with a negative outcome has never been successful for me.

Recent neurological research suggests why this is so. Over the last couple of hundred years or so, most of the attention on the brain has been focused on the cortex, that is to say, the human brain. But in the last few decades, attention has turned to other parts of the brain that hadn't been accessible in the past. In particular, we have been looking at the mammal brain and the limbic system, as well as the reptile brain, which we all have and which sits just under the mammal brain. These mammal and reptile brains are not very smart, but they are very quick and they make a lot of noise. They are also hooked to the rest of the body and when they get excited, they can get the whole body in a considerable uproar with the blood pumping and adrenaline levels up and so on.

So if I tell the audience a story with an unhappy ending, for instance, "That company that went bankrupt because it didn't implement knowledge management!" what seems to be happening is that this ancient part of the brain, the limbic system, kicks in and the message is: "Trouble! Something bad is happening! Do something! Fight! Flight!" Now the human brain, the cortex, can intervene and override these primitive organs and in effect say something like, "Now calm down, reptile brain, let's analyze this. We may be able to learn something from this unfortunate but instructive experience." But by the time the commotion is over, and the body has gotten back to normal, the opportunity to invent a new future may have passed. Learning may take place, but no rapid action ensues. There is no springboard effect. The cortex is recovering from another encounter with the reptile brain.

But by contrast, if I tell a story with a happy ending, what seems to be happening is that the limbic system kicks in with something called an "endogenous opiate reward" for the human brain, the cortex. It pumps a substance called dopamine into the cortex. Basically, it puts the human brain on drugs. This leads to "a warm and floaty feeling," the kind of mildly euphoric feeling that you have after you have just seen a wonderful movie. And this is the perfect frame of mind to be thinking about a new future, a new identity for yourself or your organization.

The Storyteller Has to Let Go of Control

There are other limitations to getting the springboard effect. One is that you have to let go of control. Suppose I tell you stories like Zambia or Madagascar and then I go on to say, "And now this is what it means for you in your unit. Let me tell you what you have to do tomorrow morning." Then, I am right back in the command-and-control mode. So I have to stand back to a certain extent and trust that the story will ignite the listeners' own creativity. And I have to have the self-control to avoid imposing my views on the listener. I am not in a battle to impose my idea. I have to let the listeners make up their own minds. This is hard to do. Imposing order is bred into us. So giving up control is not a trivial thing, particularly if you have been a manager for many years and have been in the habit of giving directions and making decisions and taking charge.

Some Groups Are Immune

There are some groups on whom this kind of storytelling doesn't work very well. Old-style Soviets or accountants can be a problem. Anyone in fact who is intent on imposing their view of the world on others will immediately sense in this kind of a story a quickening of the pulse and a spurt of energy and a vision of a different kind of organization, and will at once sense that some kind of destabilizing virus is entering the environment. Warning signals go off in the brain that there is a risk of unpredictability, a risk of loss of control. For the freedom-lover, this will be welcome. But the control-minded person will typically set out to find and resist the virus in order to reestablish control and predictability. Usually they can't find the virus, because they never suspect that the destabilizing element could possibly be anything as simple and innocuous as a mere story. They know that stories are ephemeral and subjective and anecdotal and are not to be taken seriously. But they themselves may resist the spell of the story for their own conduct, because they sense that something is amiss in their calm and controlled world. And so a springboard story doesn't necessarily work on everyone. With some groups, you don't get the "spring."

The Storyteller Must Believe

For the story to have the springboard effect, it has to be performed with feeling. It has to be performed with passion. The storyteller must tell the story as though she had actually lived the experience herself, as though she had been that task team leader in Madagascar, desperate to get the answer to a difficult question. This is because what is rubbing off on the listeners is not just the intellectual content of the story: it is the feeling in the story that is communicated to the listener. It is the emotion that makes the connection between the storyteller and the listener. This is what catches the listeners' attention, and gives the story its "spring" and pushes the listeners to reinvent a new story in their own contexts, and fill in the gaps to make it happen.

The Marriage of Narrative and Analysis

It is important to keep in mind that storytelling is not a panacea. I am not saying to forget about analysis of costs and benefits and risks and timelines and all the structural things that you will need to do to implement a complex idea in a large organization. What I am saying is: do all the analysis, but use the narrative to get people *inside* the idea, so that they *live* the idea, so that they *feel* the idea, so that they *understand* how the idea might work. And once they are *inside* the idea, and once they have felt it and understood it, then you can move on and share with them the analysis.

So you marry the narrative with the analysis. Once listeners have lived the idea through a story, they are able to perform the analysis in a more balanced way, looking at both costs and benefits. Often the analysis that is performed on new ideas in organizations is focused on the costs and risks and difficulties, the disruptions and dislocations, because that is what people are immediately aware of when they hear about something that will require change. It often happens that the analysts fail to think through what the benefits might be, because they are so preoccupied with the negative side of the equation. A story can help listeners analyze both costs and benefits in an even-handed manner.

Finding the Right Story

People often ask me: how do you find the right story? What I did at the World Bank was to wander around the organization and ask people for examples where the kind of change I wanted had already happened, at least in part. In fact, I never "found" a story lying there, like a stone on the path that I could just pick up and use. What I found was not a complete ready-to-perform story. Instead, what I found were more like leads. I would find fragments that might be turned into stories.

For instance, when I first heard about that Madagascar story, it was an e-mail describing a small part of the eventual story, and I rejected it. I said to myself, "That will never work. It doesn't have this. It doesn't have that. It doesn't have the elements that I need." Initially, I couldn't see the story that would eventually emerge. But then I ran out of leads. I ended up rejecting all of the potential leads that I had on hand. And so I went back to the reject pile and started asking more questions about these leads, including the e-mail about Madagascar. "Was anything else going on when you got that answer?" I asked. And so it turned out that there was more than one piece of advice. "Oh yes, there was the retired guy." And then when I asked further, I heard, "And oh yes, there was professor from Toronto." And so finally I began to see how I might weave these leads into a story. Once I had enough material to do a story, then I had to perfect it. The way that story sounds now is not the way it sounded when I first tried to tell it. When an audience hears it now, it sounds as though that's the only way to tell it. But there were many test runs. It's only through practice that you get the story to come out right.

We Are All Storytellers

Who can be a springboard storyteller? Who can get this springboard effect? Does it require special talents or background? I was walking out of a presentation at a conference a while back, following some participants who didn't realize that I was right behind them. I heard one say to his colleague, "You know this was all very interesting, but it's no use to me. I couldn't tell a story if my life depended on it. So this storytelling tool is no use to me. I am not a storyteller."

By way of reply, I'd like to cite my wife who considers my actitivies as a storyteller somewhat ironic. She says, "This is crazy. Look at yourself, Steve. Monosyllabic. Quiet. Reserved. Never saying a word at the dinner table. Never regaling me with stories. But here you are going round the world, apparently making a living out of telling stories, and now what's worse, teaching others how to tell stories. If you can tell stories, anybody can!"

And indeed that's the point. We are all storytellers. We spend most of our lives, wittingly or unwittingly, telling stories. In fact, it's not something we have to learn, it's something we do, day in and day out, every day. It's something that we are able to do at the age of 2. Jerome Bruner has documented how little children at this age, as soon as they can start to talk, show that they understand the stories that their families tell them, and they start to tell their own stories, and also start to tell stories to themselves as part of their first efforts to make sense of their lives. It happens so easily and so spontaneously and so pervasively that some scientists believe that storytelling is hard-wired into our brains.

It is only several years later that we start having abstract language beaten into our brains by schoolteachers and the education system. Abstract language doesn't occur spontaneously in children. It is something that they have to be systematically taught. Given the struggle that most of us have to master abstract reasoning, it seems unlikely that it is hard-wired in our brains. It has to be learned. And most of us do learn it, but with an immense effort, almost like learning a foreign language. Abstract concepts have to be taught to us, and it is generally a slow, hard process. Some of us eventually get quite good at this abstract language, this foreign language. But whenever we get a chance, whenever we are relaxing with our friends, or outside of school or work, we lapse back into our native language of narrative at the first opportunity. We are at home in our native language of storytelling. When we exchange stories, we find ourselves refreshed. It is energizing, unlike the foreign language of abstractions, which most of us find so tiring. So why not communicate with people in their native language?

Becoming a Better Storyteller

So everyone can tell stories. Everyone already knows how to tell stories, since we do it every day of our lives, even if we are as unaware of it as fish may be unaware of the water they swim in.

What often happens, though, when you ask someone to tell a story in front of an audience, is that there is a tendency to freeze, and the speaker becomes tongue-tied, and forgets what he or she knows how to do very well. It is like asking someone to describe how to ride a bicycle or throw a ball. We are all able to do this, but we have difficulty explaining how we do it. And if asked to perform it after being required to provide an explanation, we may become self-unconscious and momentarily forget how to do something that we already know.

It's also the case that stories have been so disparaged for several thousand years, ever since Plato's Republic, that we usually haven't thought much about using stories for a serious purpose. Once we understand that how stories work and how they can be used to achieve a useful purpose, then we can start to use our natural talents as storytellers and focus them in new and more effective ways to get specific results.

And we can all get better at storytelling. Much better. Particularly at using stories intelligently and explicitly to get effects that we explicitly plan for and intend. As in any field of human activity, understanding how and why storytelling works, and learning what kinds of stories work in different situations, and what kinds of effects different kinds of stories have, can enable us to be more adept in our own practice of storytelling.

But the main way to improve our ability to tell stories is of course to practice. Practice, practice, practice, and then more practice. And find a safe space to practice. You don't want to be telling a story for the first time to the executive committee of a large organization, because it is likely to have some unexpected effects.

When I told the Madagascar story to the senior management of the World Bank in January 2000, I had already told the story many times to different audiences, and in the process, I had refined and honed and perfected the story so that it had exactly the effect that I intended with a wide range of different listeners. When I told the story in that high-profile high-risk situation, I was extremely confident that it would have the effect that it did. And of course, that confidence in knowing the story well also helps the storyteller to be convincing and effective in telling the story.

So practice, practice, practice, particularly in low-risk situations. One can do this with a friend, or a colleague, or a spouse, until one is comfortable with the performance.

Once one has mastered the technique, one can relax as the story-teller and simply enjoy the performance. All the tension of presenting abstract material tends to disappear because there are none of the adversarial implications of trying to get the listener to accept *my* analysis of the situation. Storytelling is like a dance, in which I invite the listeners to come with me, arm-in-arm, and together we explore a story. It is as though the storyteller and the listener are walking down a path together exploring and co-creating the setting and the trajectory of the story. Whether anything comes of it will depend, not on the story that I tell, but rather on the story that the listeners tell themselves. It is *their own* story that will be liberating, energizing, and exciting.

Stephen Denning: Reflections

When we organized the original Smithsonian Associates' symposium in April 2001, we felt that the event could well have lasting consequences. It has certainly had lasting consequences for me.

THE GROWTH OF ORGANIZATIONAL STORYTELLING

The symposium led to my becoming involved on a full-time basis in the emerging world of organizational storytelling. When I left the World Bank in December of 2000, I assumed that, since I was known in the field of knowledge management, that people would be interested in me as an expert in knowledge management, with perhaps a bit of storytelling on the side. To my surprise it's turned out over the last 3 years that there has been more corporate interest in organizational storytelling. I had never expected that companies all around the world, including firms like GE, McDonalds, and IBM, would be interested in organizational storytelling. And The Smithsonian Associates' event in 2001 was one of the catalysts for that.

Why are they interested in storytelling? The most frequent area in which I am asked for help, is "How do I get change? How do I spark change? How do I communicate a complex new idea? How do I get people to embrace that complex new idea and get on with implementation enthusiastically and energetically? In effect, how do I take this organization by the scruff of the neck and hurl it into the future, so that everyone actually wants to be part of that future?" The kind of executives who approach me are typically people who are just below the top of the organization—people who know what's wrong, who know what to do, but somehow can't seem to connect with the people who have the control of the organization. So that is the area where there is greatest interest in getting help.

Other areas that are of interest include storytelling to build communities, and storytelling that transmits values. After Enron and the other corporate scandals, people can see the importance of values: how do you instill in the organization the values that ensure that accounts can be trusted and that systems will be failsafe? But the most important area is that of getting change: how do you persuade people to change? That's the principal reason that people come to me for help, and generally it's because they've tried everything else and nothing else works. Often they're at the end of the road, and they're desperate, just as I was, back in 1996, and willing to try anything.

An Example of the Use of Organizational Storytelling

In my work, I've seen a number of examples of the successful use of storytelling to effect change in an organization. One was with a major oil company in which one of the senior engineers was trying to persuade the organization to implement a different way of building a deep-sea well, a way of building it in 4 months instead of the usual 12 to 18 months. He had been tasked with developing this methodology, and he was expecting that when it was introduced people would say "Wow, that's terrific, let's do it!" With such capital-intensive projects, the methodology had the potential to save a great deal of money. And he thought that the case would be obvious. But it was the opposite: everyone had reasons why this thing would not and could not and should not be implemented in this particular case. I mean "Why us?" And "Where else have you tried this?" After 6 months, he actually got a decision to implement it, but he could see that if this was the way it was going to be implemented across the organization, then most of the time-savings and cost-savings were going to be lost in arguments about how and whether to do it.

He got himself put on a task force on how the company could learn faster. The task force made an interim report to their senior management about the problems they had faced and what needed to be done. But the report with the standard reasons and charts and slides didn't connect with the management. It was just another change proposal. And the task force realized that they had to reach the management on a different level: they had to grasp that the company had to be run in a different way. So they decided to make the final presentation in the form of story about the difficulties of getting the new standard methodology for building deep-sea wells accepted and how it had eventually succeeded: "But just imagine—just imagine, if we'd got on the same page on Day 1 instead of Day 183!"

When the engineer made the presentation, he was holding his breath because he knew that suggesting to management that a company should be run in a different way can be a dangerous occupation. But what happened was this: the CEO paused and said, "You know, that reminds me of when I was a young engineer." And this sparked a whole set of stories by the top management team about how they had been dealing with these kind of problems when they were earlier in their career, and there was a burst of energy—"Why don't we do this; why don't we make this happen?" And suddenly they had grasped the point: 'This means us! We have to change! We have to run this company differently." And so the whole thing took off with a lot of momentum. He was amazed at the difference between making the presentation in the regular way when it was "just another change proposal" and telling it in the form of a story and it suddenly connects with the managers on a personal level, so that it becomes their own story.

THE FIELD HAS WIDENED AND DEEPENED

Another thing that's happened since 2001 is that the whole field of organizational storytelling has widened and deepened, both for me and for everyone. I was talking in *The Springboard,* and at the Smithsonian symposium itself, about one highly valuable kind of organizational storytelling. But since then, I've come across at least six other kinds of storytelling that are highly useful in business. Back in April 2001, it wasn't so clear to me that the different purposes one might have in telling stories have different types of narrative patterns associated with them. And much of my time and energy in the last year has been spent in delineating these different narrative patterns—how they work and why they work, why they're different from each other. It's now much clearer to me that understanding the differences between the patterns can dramatically enhance your chances of telling a story that will have the effect that you intend.

Many of the mistakes that I see in people trying to use storytelling as tool for leadership is that they don't understand the different patterns associated with different purposes. So they read the *Harvard Business Review* and they conclude that "storytelling's hot" and then they think, "Well, I'll try telling a story." But if they haven't thought through what kind of a story and the purpose of telling it, then there is a significant risk that they'll end up with a story with the wrong pattern.

For instance, they'll tell a negative story with the object of trying to get people into action. Suppose they're trying to introduce knowledge management, they might tell a story in the form, "I know a firm that went bankrupt because it didn't implement knowledge management." That kind of story is a typical first stab at this, but basically it's highly unlikely to get people moving rapidly into action to adopt knowledge management, because its tone is negative.

To get people into action you need to reverse the tonality and turn it into a positive springboard story: "I know a firm that solved its problem by implementing knowledge management." This is not to say that the story about the firm that went bankrupt can't be a useful story for imparting knowledge and understanding about knowledge management. But it's not very likely to get people rapidly into action, for which you need a story with a positive tone. So, this has led from "Storytelling 101," where people start to see the importance of storytelling for leadership in organizations, to "Storytelling 102," where they start to examine the different purposes for which you can use storytelling in organizations and the different patterns of narrative that correspond to those purposes.

The Limits of Storytelling's Effectiveness

A question that I'm asked frequently is: does storytelling work in every part of the world? Is this culturally specific? My take is that there are cultural differences, but they are much less significant than the similarities. We have yet to find a culture that does not revolve around storytelling. It may exist, but we haven't found it yet. Different cultures do have different emphases.

For instance, there are studies showing that on average men respond better to images and women to words.[9] It has also been suggested that people from Asia respond more holistically to communications, whereas people in the West tend to look at the issues piece by piece.[10] These studies suggest differences, but the much more important point is that all cultures revolve around stories. There are some nuances or emphases in some cultures, and certain types of stories flourish more in some cultures than in others. But the deeper message is that stories flourish everywhere.

Digital Storytelling

A different question that's sometimes asked has to do with the effectiveness of storytelling via e-mail or other virtual communication media. If you're sharing information, then electronic media can do a very good job. It works as well on the Web as anywhere else, probably better. If you want a stock price, the weather report, a train timetable—these things you can get on the Web easily and quickly and accurately, and it's wonderful. It has certainly simplified life a great deal, having quick access to information like that. But if you're getting into deeper kinds of questions, if you're doing what I'm trying to do—persuade a change-resistant organization to change; if you're trying to talk to people who, when you start communicating with them aren't interested at all in what you have to say, then you're in a different ballgame. I've not seen virtual communications able to deal at all with that kind of a situation. I've not seen any instance where anyone has been able to effect significant change with a skeptical audience by sending an e-mail and asking people to visit a website. And the reason is that it's difficult to do anyway. Even if you're there in person, it's going to be a difficult challenge. But if you're not there in person, it's not really possible.

For one thing there isn't enough bandwidth. Studies have been done showing what is the impact of storytelling and where does it come from. These studies indicate that somewhere around 10 percent of the communication comes from the content, and around 90 percent comes from the tone of voice, the gesture, the look in the eye, and all of that. In virtual communication you're missing most of that 90 percent—you're dealing with the 10 percent, and there simply isn't enough bandwidth to connect with the person, to make it happen.

Another aspect is that storytelling in person is intensely interactive, whereas virtual communication is passive. When you tell a story in person, you get all sorts of cues in terms of expressions and body language from the audience as to how they are responding to the story, and you adjust the story to take that into account. In a virtual encounter, that kind of feedback is absent and so the experience becomes something very different.

I'm not saying you can't get a lot of information from the Web. I am a great fan of the Web and it's wonderful; but if you're trying to do something difficult like take a change-resistant organization up by the scruff of the neck and hurl it into the future, then I've got a very simple, two-word piece of advice: Be there!

CHAPTER ENDNOTES

1 Walden.

2 Some examples from the period at the start of the 21st century were: the head of Mattel lasted 37 months; Lucent, 36 months; Campbell Soup, 33 months; Coca-Cola, 28 months; Covad, 28 months; Procter & Gamble, 17 months; Maytag, 15 months; Xerox, 13 months.

3 Sun-Tzu: *The Art of War* (trans. Ralph D. Sawyer. Westview, 1994).

4 These might include for instance, knowledge strategy, knowledge leadership, communities of practice, help desks, knowledge bases, knowledge capture, knowledge storage, knowledge authentication, knowledge dissemination, knowledge taxonomies, quality assurance, procedures for removing obsolete knowledge, budget, incentives, and measurement.

5 George Steiner, *Grammars of Creation* (New Haven, Yale University Press, 2001) page 85. An early reference to it lies in Plato's Theaetetus, Plato, *The Theaetetus of Plato* (trans. M.J. Levett, Hackett, Indianapolis, 1990) where thoughts are likened to birds in an aviary. There is an excellent discussion in Sven Birkerts, in *The Gutenberg Elegies: The Fate of Reading in an Electronic Age*, (Boston, Faber and Faber, 1994).

6 Jeffrey Pfeffer and Robert I. Sutton, *The Knowing-Doing Gap: How Smart Companies Turn Knowledge into Action* (Boston, Harvard Business School Press, 2000).

7 Stephen Denning, *The Springboard: How Storytelling Ignites Action in Knowledge-Era Organizations* (Boston, Butterworth & Heinemann, 2000) page 165.

8 Groh Productions: *The Art of Possibility*, with Ben Zander.

9 Neurological research indicating that women concentrate more on verbal information in each film and men focus more on the visual content can be found summarized at: "QEEG Correlates of Film Presentations: Experiment 2: Gender effects in topographic EEG" at http://www.skiltopo.com/papers/applied/articles/dakdiss4.htm March 8, 2004.

10 Richard Nisbett: *The Geography of Thought: How Asians and Westerners Think Differently and Why* (New York, Free Press, 2003).

FIVE

Storytelling in Making Educational Videos

The real voyage of discovery consists not in seeking new landscapes, but in having new eyes.

—Marcel Proust

Katalina Groh's Original Presentation

In the previous chapter, Steve Denning talked about the role of storytelling in his work as a change agent in large organizations. In this chapter, I talk about the function of storytelling in my role as the chief executive of a small film production company, Groh Productions, that makes educational videos. My current series, *Real People, Real Stories*™ includes *The Art of Possibility*, a video about Ben Zander, the orchestra conductor.

AN ABSURD IDEA: AN EDUCATION FILM SERIES ON STORYTELLING

When Steve Denning sent me his book, I began reading it and I started laughing on the very first page. It opened with a quote from Albert Einstein:

> *"If the idea at first is not absurd, then there is no hope for it."*

I liked that because it was the week that I was launching the series, *Real People, Real Stories*™. Everyone thought it was a very strange idea for a video series. It was going to 75 countries in 35 languages. I was unsure what the global education market would think about a whole series explicitly devoted to storytelling.

And yet it's had the most successful first 3-month release from this distributor in 15 years. People have been buying it without even previewing it, or even asking to preview it, before it came out. So it's received a strong response even though it's something different.

LESSONS LEARNED FROM MAKING FILMS

Let me tell you about some of the discoveries we have made in making films. This is an ongoing process. We make our films now very differently from the way we made them just a year ago. Some of the best discoveries we made were when we heard comments like, "This doesn't work because of that." You hear what's not working for some reason for somebody. So you ask: "What's the barrier?" We're always trying to overcome the barriers to understanding.

What's the "So What?"

It sounds elementary that films need to have a purpose. But it's something that we have to keep asking ourselves, especially when we have a lot of entertaining material. I learned this first when I was making a film on collaboration technologies. We had just had a big long shoot for the film. There was a lot of excitement and there were wonderful stories. The interviews had gone well. I felt it was a big success. And at the time, we had hired a consultant, Michael Schrage, who was helping us with the content. I had sent him stacks of transcripts, and I was thinking to myself, "With all this wonderful stuff, we're on our way!"

I'll never forget what Michael said to me. I was on the telephone with him and he was outside a conference, about to give a talk. He's always very busy. He said to me, "Katalina, I've read all the stuff and have comments, but I've only got 15 minutes."

When he said that, I first got quiet. Although I did not know him long, I had learned that he doesn't hold anything back. He said, "Yeah actually though, I don't really need 15 minutes. I don't even need 1 minute." And now I began laughing, because I knew he was going to say something awful. But I still wanted his help in getting us on the right track.

He said: "I've read all of the stuff, all of these stories from all of these people. These are great transitions and great stories. But none of it answers the most important question of all: so what?" There was a pause and then he said, "OK? Got to go."

I said, "Bye!"

And I sat there. I knew immediately that he was right. It didn't matter how wonderful these stories were. We weren't making a discursive documentary for public television. We had a very tough audience. We would have people asking, "Why am I buying this to show to my organization? What are they going to get out of it?" They needed to have an answer to the question, "So what?" It was an important discovery for us.

The Difficult Part: Distilling the Essence

One of the most difficult aspects of making a film is deciding what to leave in the video. After we had spent weeks doing the Zander video, researching it, and doing nine film shoots, with several cameras, we had many hours of footage from which we were going to cut a 26-minute film. When we were editing the film, John Seely Brown offered to come by and look at the material with our two editors and help with the content editing and offer some input on what content might be most valuable to our audience. At first, he was excited and said things like, "Oh such great stuff!" And then, as we saw more and more footage, his attitude changed. I wouldn't say that he was upset. Rather he was consumed by the volume of it, and he would say things like, "What are we going to do with all of this?"

And that's the question we always come back to: what are we trying to do? There are a lot of great stories within any one project. But the point is that it has to be more than a set of stories. We have to be careful that this isn't just something that's fun to look at, something entertaining about a great music teacher. What you choose to keep and why you keep it comes from answering the question over and over, "What will our audience connect to, and why should they care?" Then we take all of the content story pieces that we have chosen to keep, and we move them around until they are no longer only a collection of content sections and individual stories, but combine to become elements of an all-new greater narrative.

The Emotional Punch-Line of the Story

People often ask me, "How do we create a narrative in a video?" We try to make it entertaining, and not just entertaining in the sense of laughing or enjoying it. There are amusing and enjoyable parts to these films, with songs and jokes and so on. But these films have more—they have what Larry Prusak in an earlier chapter called emotional punch. This is the most important element in a good story, whether it's told through a film or whether it's told orally or whether it's written in a book. It doesn't matter whether it's a happy emotion, or a violent emotion like the cultural stories of blood and murder that Larry mentioned, or whether it's sad or funny, it has to have an emotional punch-line. Hopefully it has many emotional punch-lines, because the emotional punch-line is what keeps the audience engaged. So we always focus a good deal on creating emotional transitions.

Telling Stories Differently—to Different Audiences

As the chief executive of a small film production company, I tell stories every day. That's virtually all I do. Whether I'm playing producer or playing director or being the script-writer or trying to get people to put up money for a film, I'm always telling stories.

When I am working with a musician to get them to play something for us with a particular feeling, it's no surprise that I can, and usually do, talk with them for hours at a time. As artists, they are storytellers and if they are great musicians, they tell stories with their music. But having their attention for long periods of time is not difficult. It's normal. Working with other artists is simply a part of what I do, and in many ways not always the most important. While musicians and filmmakers will share stories for hours while discussing their collaborations, sometimes my audience will listen to me for about 30 seconds before they decide whether they want to hear any more.

At other times, I know I've got a willing audience. We may have a meeting of an hour and a half, where people have just had lunch, and they're very relaxed. That's one kind of storytelling.

That's very different from telling a story in a 1-minute conversation to try to get someone interested in putting up money for a film. This is often the most important story that I tell, since the film won't get made without the money. That brief conversation and the story that I tell the distributor are key. For instance, a little while back, when I was working on a different project, I had a phone call with the president of a large cable company. He's precisely the kind of person I need because he can get the film out to a mass audience so that many people will see it. In some ways he's the most important person for us, since we obviously want the film to reach an audience.

So I called this president of the large cable company. In fact, we had a scheduled call and I was surprised at that time to have gotten that far with a film not yet finished. Although I was slightly surprised that he took my call at all, I thought I was fully prepared. I had lots of notes. And of course I had many things that I planned to tell him. But we were only on the phone for 15 seconds after brief introductions when he cut me off and said, "Well, I bet you have a great story."

I laughed and said, "Yes, I do."

And then he came back with, "OK, let's hear it."

I took a deep breath and was just about to begin with what I planned would be a long-winded hour-long story, which of course I believed to be the greatest story. But before I said even one word this cable president cut me off with two words. He said, "Two sentences."

I didn't say a word for a moment, but then managed, "Two sentences?"

He came back with a snappy, "If you can't tell me your story in two sentences, then how would we know what to write in the television show directory that would make audiences choose to watch this film over everything else they can watch?"

I was silent and a bit panicked. Strangely though, although he was being so abrupt, I was not annoyed by his surprise guideline but in fact I thought to myself, "Of course! How stupid I am not to have thought of it. My heart raced, trying to think quickly of something fabulous to say in two sentences, when I was accustomed to having as much time as I wanted to tell my story. Words, parts of sentences, pieces of thoughts, all flashed around in front of my eyes but they were fragments. I knew I had to say something quickly and still try to sound fabulous and intriguing. In a couple moments, I finally managed to take a yet new breath and begin with, "Well..."

Again he cut me right off but this time sarcastically with, "Is 'Well' *really*, the first word of your first sentence?"

At this point I just started laughing. I knew I wouldn't impress this guy, and it was clear I was choking. So I confessed, "Asking for the story in only two sentences is a really great question, I just never thought of it." He liked that I did not get upset or mad. My laughter changed everything.

He laughed too and said, "Actually Katalina, I'm not a mean guy. It is just that you have to let me know right from the beginning that you can describe your story to your audience in two sentences, because that's all they'll read in the television guide. If you can't make the story good in two sentences, you're not ready to talk with me."

He said, "I'll believe you have a good story. I trust you have a good story. But call me tomorrow at noon, when you have it in two sentences. OK?"

And I said OK and hung up.

But what could have been a disaster turned into something quite the opposite. Luckily, instead of becoming upset during my failed storytelling attempt, I laughed—so then he laughed. I got off our less than 1-minute phone call shocked and humbled, but energized. I realized that I was lucky to have another chance. And most importantly, I realized that I had just learned something very important about telling stories.

Of course, I was ready for that call with him the next day, armed with a plan. What were the two sentences that I told him the next day? When he answered the call, I could actually hear the smile in his voice when he said, "Well Katalina, I bet you have two very good sentences today."

I said, and this was key: "Actually, I have only one sentence." He started laughing. We both did, and he said slowly, "Very good." I ended up with just one sentence to describe my film. And this was the sentence: "It's a very American story about what it means to be from someplace else."

It must have been the right sentence, because we ended up talking for an hour on the phone. But not so simply. The storytelling dance started very slowly. When I had given him my one single sentence, I just waited. There was silence, but I didn't interrupt it. After a pause, he said, "Good. OK, give me one more."

And so then I gave him another single sentence, just like he wanted, and then I waited, again. After a couple of minutes of this strange but also interesting dance, we finally began to simply converse back and forth, in a "normal" way. We had a lively laughing and energizing conversation.

In fact, that day, the cable television president apologized to me. He said, "Look, I'm sorry I was abrupt yesterday. I hope you don't think I'm a jerk."

I said, "No." I couldn't expect that he was going to have a lot of time for me simply because I happened to think that my story was so grippingly interesting.

When I had come back to him the next day with one sentence instead of the requested two, now, I was talking in *his* language. I was respecting the way *he* wanted to hear the story. Instead of being angry about being cut off, I realized that he was just different, and our shared laughter actually created a bond between us, which had happened in about a minute. I realized that he did want to hear my story, but he wanted to hear it in *his way*, which actually meant he wanted to take it from me piece by piece. Yes, at first it was odd, but so what? It was his way, and that is OK. In the end, it was very interesting because I discovered immediately that I had to give him 100 percent of the control and power of the conversation—*of the way*—the story, my story, would be told to him. But then in the end, he had given it back to me when I realized that the story had made him feel something inside that he shared back with me. I had given it away, gladly, but then it came back.

At first, I had to find out what he cared about. And what he cared about was, "What am I going to put into the ad for the people who might watch this video?" That was his priority. Once I'd provided him with that, the conversation could move on.

But the conversation could only move on in a good way, if he led it, and if he took the story from me. This was a powerful discovery. I would give him one line to begin and then wait, until he asked me a question; then, I would give him another line in the story. For this powerful executive, being in control of how to hear what he wanted to hear was part of the process, for it to work. And, it was OK. It was different, but it was OK. Because what happened after that became another powerful discovery.

As we talked, he asked more questions about the film, and after a while it turned out that he had many personal reasons for identifying with the story and the film. We talked for a long time, but not because my film's story was the most amazing thing he had ever heard. It was because we were able to discuss *his* story, instead of just *my* story, that we ended up talking for over an hour. In fact, this busy executive sounded a bit reluctant to end the call. Why? Not because my unfinished film was the best thing around, but because he did not want the experience he was having in the sharing of stories that were personal to him, to end. It is really so simple.

That's also the reason why he asked me to send him the rough cut when it was ready. He became engaged in a conversation that was based on his personal experiences, on his personal story. It was sparked by *my* story but ended up being about *his* story.

Discovering the audience's story, that's what we're always trying to achieve with these films. I realized that being able to be a storyteller in business, was every bit if not more important that being one with film crews or musicians. This executive had asked for two sentences, and so I gave him one. I played his game, and why not? I spoke his language and respected his rules of storytelling, and I adopted them for our future conversations. He had his own way of communicating, his own language, but I had to *hear it*, not be offended by it, and then adapt to it. And it had to be genuine; he was too smart to know if I was pretending. But by genuinely listening and realizing that he needed to take the story from me, for it to work the result was then an energizing and productive shared experience— one I will never forget. And the most valuable discovery was the most important one of all—it was realizing that every person has a different way they hear a story—a different way to be engaged, to experience, and that *none of them are wrong*.

So what we are trying to do is to hear and feel intuitively what this person responds to when we tell a story, because our goal is the same—we want our story to create an experience for them so that we will discover the audience's story—whether the audience is watching our film or working on one of them or the audience is an executive that we hope will show it to the world.

Stories by Different People for Different People

Many people work together to produce a successful video. I'm the producer and I start out with a concept. But there are many others involved, including focus groups with about 30 to 40 people looking at the film at different stages while we're making it.

When we show the film to an audience, I enjoy hearing the reactions of the audience, because they are so diverse. I enjoy learning what people learned from it and what it made them think about. In fact, we learn the most from hearing seemingly negative responses of the kind, "This is not what it's like at work!" or "This is misleading! We are not musicians! The environment of Ben Zander, the music conductor, is not the environment that we're in!" We always learn a great deal from these responses, because these reactions help us realize that we have so many different audiences that we are creating the stories for.

Storytelling Is Interactive

How does one learn how to tell a story? As Steve Denning said in the previous chapter, it's a matter of practice. When it doesn't go right the first time, or the tenth time, then of course, you have to keep trying and doing something different.

A key is knowing where to begin the story. I discovered that the story usually shouldn't begin at the chronological beginning. You have to tell the story so that it relates to what the listener cares about. How do you know what the listener cares about? It's an intuitive thing, and it's practice. You have to try it, because in the process you move from what might just barely spark their interest to what really gets them engaged. To achieve this, you tell the story so that you become interactive as soon as possible.

As Larry Prusak said in an earlier chapter, it's not like the Monty Python approach to learning, where you open up someone's head and you pour the knowledge in. You're waiting for the audience to respond, to come back to you. Because the sooner the audience responds, whether it's hundreds of people watching a video at the same time, or whether I'm speaking to a single individual, the sooner the audience experiences the story and really feels something with their own story, the better the story is. That's the objective—to have the audience experience stories of their own.

Everybody Has a Story!

One of the first discoveries I made was during the making of a documentary film called "Debbie's Way." To help me prepare for the film, they had given me about 20 tapes. I liked only 2 of them. Both of those 2 tapes were reality-based. They were true-life stories. I didn't know it at the time, but that's what I liked about these programs.

In the first interviews that we did for this film, we discovered that everybody had a story. And the best story didn't come from the chief executive officer of the company. It came from an obscure person that nobody suspected would be a great storyteller. We ended up focusing the film on her, because she was such a natural storyteller. So we discovered that somebody who's not saying a lot may have the most interesting story. This discovery guided our interviewing and research. And it changed the way we made the film. We now know that no matter how we start our initial outline, it is going to change during the making of the film. We have learned to feel more comfortable with the inevitability of change, and with the fact that we are going to lose whole masses of work. We have to have the courage to dump what we've done and move on.

The Most Unlikely Person Can Be a Storyteller

One of the most exciting things about storytelling is to realize that this is something that anyone can do. I am more and more convinced how powerful the phenomenon is, realizing that everyone has a story, and watching the way the story goes back and forth between people when stories are being shared.

I'm also an unlikely storyteller. If you'd met me 15 years ago, you would have seen that I was the quietest, shyest person. I didn't even speak English until I went to school, because we only spoke Hungarian at home. I was born in the United States, but I didn't even understand English for the first 2 years of school. I just sat there listening. I didn't know what was going on. I went home and we spoke Hungarian. So it took a long time since I didn't talk to anyone else at home in English. It was hard for me to communicate at school with my heavy Hungarian accent, and so I was very quiet. I lived through years of feeling as though I had something to say, but I never said it. And what helped me was when I had some teachers who pulled it out of me and got me to start. They thought, "She must have something to say." And now, I'm helping other people tell their stories.

People Learn from a Story

The next big light bulb that went off for us was in 1995. It was another accident. We were making educational films, and we would have four or five bulleted points that we were hoping that people would learn. We were spending our time focusing on the precise wording of those bulleted points. What we discovered almost by accident was that the wording hardly mattered. The only points people remembered 1 or 2 weeks later were the points that had been embodied in a story. So if we told a great story, then people remembered the point. Otherwise not. We found that when people would come to a meeting a couple of weeks later, they'd completely forgotten the bulleted points, but they could repeat the story back to us almost verbatim. Through following the story, they knew what they were supposed to have learned. That was a powerful discovery.

Eliciting a Story Through Telling a Story

Another stage was realizing how to get people to tell us a story. The best stories didn't come from asking people questions, because people would almost unconsciously answer questions in response to what they thought we wanted to hear. Instead, we found that it worked better if we told our own stories, and then they would tell their own personal stories. In this way, it was no longer a matter of question-and-answer. It was going back and forth, exchanging stories. In this mode, they weren't telling me what they thought I wanted to hear. They were telling me a story that contained what they really thought and felt.

When the film came out, it was a small reality-based 17-minute film, unlike anything else that was on the market. It ended up doing well. It was reviewed and it got a lot of publicity because of the power of her storytelling. But the storytelling was still subtle and in the background. In the current series of films, like *The Art of Possibility* with Ben Zander, the series is explicitly about storytelling.

Storytelling Can Engage Even a Busy Audience

The next step was when we launched the film series on collaborative technologies. One day we had a meeting with 30 or 40 people—all very busy people—who had come together for 1 hour over lunch to look at a half-hour film. I proposed that they talk for about 45 minutes after seeing the film. Initially, they all said that they had places to go to or meetings to attend, and some said they couldn't even stay for lunch. They said they'd look at the film and leave, and maybe e-mail me something later. It was clear that no one had time to be there, and they were just coming as a favor for me. So they came, and we taped the discussion that followed, which ended up lasting

4½ hours. Nobody left. All these extraordinarily busy people wouldn't leave. Finally I was the one who had to say, "I'm sorry. We've got to stop."

When at last they had left, we realized that no one could agree on what the film was about. Everyone had a different idea about it. The discussion went back and forth, and we saw that we would have to throw out all of the work we had done because we weren't in the right place.

When we looked at the tapes of the discussion, we saw that these people were arguing, almost fighting. The reason it became so passionate was that people were telling their own stories. These people who were so busy, who had no time to sit there and be mere passive observers of a film, suddenly found that they had a lot of time when they were personally involved. Once they could share their own experiences and tell their own stories, then they were able to make the time.

People Learn Through Their Own Stories

Some of my staff were very upset. They were saying, "Oh my god, what happened? We've lost control."

But I was laughing and thinking, "This is wonderful!" even though everything had to be thrown out. I could see that the audience cared. They could relate to the material. Everyone had had something to say. It didn't matter that they didn't agree. It was more important that they were talking and thinking and telling stories. A lot of learning was occurring when they were arguing. They would all go home and think about it.

And this turned out to be true. They kept in touch with us. They would call me and ask, "When are we going to see the next tape?" They became very involved. It didn't matter that they didn't agree. It mattered more that they were thinking about it and talking about it and discussing it and sharing their stories. The lack of closure ended up being a good thing.

Telling the Story in the First Person—Being Authentic

I am currently making a new documentary feature film. When we started out, it was going to be a story about my parents being imprisoned in Hungary, and seeing the KGB prison just outside Budapest, from which they had escaped many years ago, and following the escape route to America. The film had a lot of action ideas. We had prisons. We had chases. We had journeys. We had these great action sequences for the film.

But now it's become something very different from that. It's now become a film about going home. Until recently, we have been calling it: *Simple Dignity: A Very American Story About What It Means to Be from Somewhere Else.*

One of the key lessons from this film was learning how to talk about the film. When I started on the film, I was writing it in the third person. It was a film about two people who happened to be my parents, but I did not say they were my parents. It was a film about a young couple being arrested and put in prison, about why they were imprisoned, about how they escaped, and about their journey to get to America. We shot in five prisons that no one had ever filmed in before. We traced the escape route through three countries as they walked to find the Americans. In the end, it took them 12 years to get to America. I was writing the story in the third person because I didn't want this seen as just a family movie. I wanted it to be taken seriously. So I kept talking about it in the third person.

Writing the film in that way was a struggle for me, whereas now, it's become a film that's almost writing itself. What enabled the transformation is that I finally shifted to telling the story in the first person. I discovered this when I was speaking with a distributor about it, and the people there were somewhat interested in it, but not fully engaged with the story. But when they realized that the film was about my parents, there was a sudden shift. They said, "Why didn't you say so?" They felt I wasn't telling the story in a way that was natural to tell it or authentic. I was telling it in what I thought was the right way. When

I had started the project I was not secure enough in myself as a storyteller to tell it in an authentic way, I was doing what I thought was "the right way," to be taken seriously. I assumed that the story itself, without my own role in it as storyteller, was so interesting that it would be a serious film story. But the discovery came when I realized that people I told it to reacted differently and much more powerfully when they discovered that the couple in the film was my parents. When I told it "the right way" it didn't involve the listener. They listened to it and they thought it was interesting. But it didn't *engage* them. It didn't elicit their own stories in a way that was personal. That only happened when I told the story in the first person. Trusting yourself to explore a story you tell is about trusting yourself to be real, to be authentic. When you are real, and then moved by what you tell, your audience will feel it immediately and respond, also, in their own authentic way.

In Telling a Story, Less Can Mean More

I also found that the less detail that I give in the story, the quicker it invites the person who's listening to tell me their story. For instance, on one occasion, we had to cut a trailer for a film. We had meetings with the executives of Sony and HBO and so on, and we suddenly needed to do a trailer in a hurry. We only had 2 days to cut the film and as a result it was going to be very rough. There would be numbers running through it, and it would look very unfinished. And most of the detail of the film would be missing.

The first time I showed the trailer, I was sitting in the office with six senior people from Sony, people who watch films all day long, just like the movie, *The Player*. They were savvy people who'd heard it all, people who'd seen it all. They were sitting around a table. I gave them a quick setup and I put in the tape and I played it. As we watched it, I was a bit worried because it looked so rough and unfinished. When the film was finished, there was a long pause. The lights were still dim. No one got up. And no one was saying anything. Just silence. I didn't know what to think. Finally a man swung around in his chair and looked at me and said, "You know, my uncle left Yugoslavia like that." For the next 45 minutes, people all told stories. I never said a word. I just listened. And these people became quite emotional, as they started to talk about things that they hadn't even thought about for a long time. These were important television executives. They *hear* stories all the time. But this one made them *tell* their own stories, stories that they'd almost forgotten. It was a huge learning experience for me. When I walked out of the meeting I called my editor as soon as I was outside. I was so excited. I was completely floating from that conversation. I told my editor, "This is it! This is what the film must do! It is not about telling our story, it is about hearing theirs." This meeting changed everything.

So the very roughness of the trailer turned out to be an unexpected plus. It worked in part because it was rough and unfinished and incomplete. It did not have an ending. The roughness, and the fact that it wasn't too detailed or finished, helped give it force, thus corroborating what Steve Denning said in the previous chapter about telling the story in a minimalist fashion.

At that time, the trailer didn't have an ending. Now, we are making a feature film, which no longer has a traditional ending, as we had originally planned. This is very unusual—cutting a 90-minute film without a traditional ending. And that's what we're doing. We're experimenting with something different. It's still full of emotional transitions and music and jokes. But it's a film with an ending that's open-ended. We learned how the audience can fill in their own ending if we don't give it to them, which can be much more powerful.

We're thinking of calling it *A Reason To Dance*. The film has already been shot on three continents, five countries. We have great photography. We have great people working on it. The footage is beautiful. And that's another part of it as well. Most of the people have worked on the film for free. They've become a big part of what the story is about. It's become their story too. We all have a reason to dance.

Why Am I Making This Film? The Marketing Process

Whether it's the distributor for the film or the audience, the task is the same: getting to the listener's story. When I'm marketing a film, I have to think through, what will the distributor care about? That means getting to his story. So there are two Katalinas. There's Katalina the warm fuzzy, passionate filmmaker coming up with new ideas at 2 o'clock in the morning in the editing room. And there's Katalina the marketer who subtly convinces the distributor that it's his own idea and that this is something that a lot of people will want to watch. If she can do that, he'll believe that this is something he wants to market and that people will watch. I can make that happen if the film makes him think about a story of his own. And when that happens, I'll say right away something like, "Really? Tell me about it!" I'm not doing that to be nice. This is key. His own story is central to the process. If he gets passionate about it, then the film is going to happen.

What Is This Film About? The Editing Process

A lot of people are involved in making a film. With one of the editors that I work with, I have great battles. When we're looking at many different stories, we often find that he wants this one and I want that one. And so we do battle. But the best things happen after we have a big battle. I have the "definites" that I want, the things that I won't give in on. There aren't too many of those. Ultimately, he'll do his best work after midnight when I leave. It might be based on what I want. Or it might be based partly on that, and partly on his own ideas. The films we made about Ben Zander were very hard to agree on because there was such an amazing amount of wonderful footage and there were many more learning content points than we could show. So I would make my case for what I wanted. And he would say, "Go away! Leave!" And then, when I would come in the next morning, we would look at what he calls, "Bachelor #1" from that old game show *The Dating Game*. And that would usually be the version I had asked for. But he would have cut several versions. Sometimes he would choose to show me "Bachelor #3" first, which is the version that *he* wanted to do, before he showed me the version I'd asked for. It's a game that we play. There is no winner. It's not about whose idea ends up being used. Most of the time we agree. Sometimes we don't. It's a process of keeping one's mind open so that we end up with what's best.

One of the most important parts of the process for finding the right stories to tell to create the most effective, finished narrative is the difficult but crucial process of knowing when to let go. Throwing out work that took a lot of time—that you also like but know might not work can be hard. My editor teaches this to me on every project. His best work is a combination of having the guts to throw out, and let go of, what is not working, even if it looks good. I am more hesitant to say goodbye to finished edited stories and tend to hold on longer. But only when you let go can you find something new, which is better, more effective and powerful. Trying different stories and ways to tell them is key to finding the best ones, but knowing when to let go of others is just as important.

The Story That's Not There But Yet Is Still There

Sometimes very good material ends up on the cutting room floor. In *The Art of Possibility* with Ben Zander, one of the stories that we fought hardest over in the editing process was a story about a wonderful violinist who always played first violin, which is the leading violinist in the orchestra who always sits in the front. One day, Zander moved her to the back of the orchestra. She was very upset about this. She became very angry and resentful and she wouldn't talk. She was furious at having been moved. She was used to being the leader on the violin section, always sitting in the front. What she ended up learning over a period of weeks is the reason why he had moved her. She discovered that even though she was in the last row, she was still leading from that last row.

It's a story that took a long time for him to tell, and it's a very good story. In the end we had to take the story out because it was too long. But what's interesting is that when people watch the film and discuss it, I'll hear someone say that that a bass player can be leading even though the bass player is never at the front of the orchestra. So even though that particular story isn't in the film, the story comes through anyway.

Radiating Possibility: Keeping the Song Going

One of the lines we wrote in *An Art of Possibility*, and probably one of the most important ideas in the film is that life is a story that we invent. Our life comprises the stories that we tell to ourselves about ourselves. These stories tell us who we are. It's our very identity. The story is who we are. We can invent the future. Our life is a story. It's a story that we can create. That is what we are trying to communicate in the video, so that's what we wrote on the cover of the new film series:

Every human being is brought into the world radiating possibility. The trick is to keep that song going.

Katalina Groh: Reflections

Grasping the Power of Storytelling

When we did the symposium, Groh Productions had already just launched a series around storytelling—and as I mentioned then, the reaction from the whole industry was "What is that? Why are you doing that?" Although they didn't laugh in my face, it was close. The idea of designing a whole series around it was met with great skepticism. scepticism. Nobody really got it. It was more like, "Uh, sure."

One of the things that I discovered from the symposium—there was such a variety of people there, so many people interested in the subject—I realized that this audience did genuinely "get it." These people were engaged, and even better they asked great questions. For the first time since launching a storytelling series, I heard great questions—the reactions were exciting then, and now after all of this time, they still are. There are several people from that symposium that I'm still in conversation with, all the time, who want to know what we're doing, and they continue to want to share what they're doing and how they're using storytelling. The number of people we have these conversations with has multiplied many times since then, but it really began there.

As I described in my talk, the way we came to the power of storytelling was an accident. How we were making those discoveries back then still shapes the way we're creating our films now. We're still looking for ideas, still wanting to create learning programs, but the difference is that we're going to create them by finding great storytellers. There are topics that people ask us to do with subjects on conflict resolution, new leaders, change, or knowing yourself. Now we are indeed finally doing a series on conflict resolution, but not because we were asked to do something on this subject, but instead because we finally found the right person. And again, by accident, not looking for it, not expecting it, we found a person who does this work and who is also a tremendous storyteller. The projects always begin when we ourselves are sparked by great stories from a great storyteller. The content must be there, but if we aren't moved by it, touched in some human way, why would our audience experience anything different? Why would they remember it long after they see it?

The growing amount of interest in our films and in narrative storytelling isn't just coming from customers in the United States, it's coming from all over the world. Our films are now in more than 80 countries. In addition, about 20 to 30% of our time now is in designing what we're calling our new "live-learning" workshops and seminars. We're creating a new group that is going to work with organizations and customers on storytelling, learning about the power of storytelling and how to do it.

LEARNING THE CUSTOMER'S STORY

We have learned a great deal from customers who are calling in and talking with us about not just how they're using our programs, but how they're trying to begin training programs or programs that use storytelling. For example, Proctor and Gamble has their own university, with programs on leadership and change and innovation. Not only are they putting hundreds of executives and other leaders through it, and using our work, but they're starting out their entire program, whether a 1-day workshop or a 3 to 4 day workshop, talking about storytelling and how they're going to be concentrating on that throughout the program.

Very soon after the symposium, the business of Groh Productions changed dramatically. We discovered that we would have to take back distribution for our own films. This changed everything. Of course, over the next year or so, we had to learn how to create an international distribution company. Not big fun, and for a while it was a hard time. However, although we were far from elated to become a day-to-day customer service business, ironically in the end it was a blessing. Piece by piece our creative people learned how to build an efficient machine that was finally running well. What's interesting is that although we were pretty darn miserable putting creative work aside to do this, nothing could have been better to help us be creative in what we are doing now. Although we weren't aware of it at the time, our view of the world as producers of our product was narrower before the symposium: we were simply storytellers back then. We recognized the value of concentrating on the power of narrative for communicating ideas and knowledge. We delivered our products to the market. We told stories, and then we told more more stories. Although we thought we were great listeners—the reality is that we weren't.

Becoming the lead distributor put us directly in contact with customers and distributors all over the world—and the real discoveries came from these countless new relationships. This never would have happened had we remained only producers. Not only did it help us grow, but also what we learned within a very short time changed everything in how we speak each day with every contact we have—whether it is our business vendor, distributor, or customer. We discovered that the real power of our growth came from becoming elicitors of our customer's stories.

In the symposium I was talking about the lens through which we saw the world. Since then, the way we see the market, the way we look at customers—the people we're making these films for—has changed completely. Instead of creating stuff and putting it out there and not really knowing how it's used, now we're speaking every day with customers who call to talk with us, to share their story. They tell us how much they like our work and come back to us with what they need, their suggestions, or their ideas for new products. And because we are hearing the stories of our customers and our distributors, we're not only able to communicate the power of narrative and storytelling, but also to hear from them how they're using it. And that's how we're learning together what we're going to do in the future with new programs.

We have also learned how powerful this is from trying it over and over, sincerely and with humility. First, we have to want to hear what they share, and, if we are sincere, they always know it. Often, they don't only purchase one product either; they come back to us to talk some more. They want to share their experiences and find out what else we can do with them. The sharing of stories and learning does not stop with the purchase; it is the beginning of a long conversation—a relationship based on a shared experience. It's interesting how quickly you can share an experience with a total stranger on the phone by sharing and hearing stories, and even more interesting that it will be remembered long after the conversation takes place. Stories are no longer just what we create on film, they influence every part of our business whether we are talking with someone in Singapore, Belgium, or Kansas City.

So our workday now includes both creative time and business time. We couldn't do our creative work the way we're doing it if the two weren't together, because we now see a bigger, fuller picture—a picture that keeps changing but with each change it gets even richer. When we get a call from a customer, whether it's about the product or to hear more about storytelling, for us it's about the same thing: *we are hearing* what they're looking for and why, and only then sharing with them what we're doing and why. And that person, whether it's a trainer, a teacher, a consultant, or a chief information officer for a Fortune 100 company—it doesn't matter who it is, and it doesn't matter if they're in the United States or in Argentina—the first thing we do is turn the conversation around and back to them. When we're talking to a customer on the phone, one of the first things we do is ask, "Who are you? How did you hear about us? Where do you live? Where are you calling from? And why are you calling us? What are you looking for?"

Even though they are always calling to ask about us, to learn about what we can sell them or teach, we do not just sell them something. Instead, every conversation is redirected first back to them. It's about hearing their story, learning their story. I don't mean to imply that every conversation becomes a lengthy conversation, in which we hear their whole life story but it could be. It doesn't have to take long to hear their story and understand why they are calling. But we do know that word-of-mouth is the number one way that people find out about us. How does this happen? We believe it comes from the continually growing web of shared experiences created by storytelling and listening. And I believe the reason our bottom line is growing is because we're genuinely interested in knowing who our customer is, why they want our product, and why they like it. It's had a huge impact on our sales.

THE RECURRING STORY OF NELSON MANDELA

Some stories keep resurfacing in conversation, whether in our studios, in our edit rooms, or with our distributors; and there's one story that reappears often. The story was about an interview I heard about 2 years ago with Nelson Mandela. He was asked how he could come out of prison after 27 years, lead his country out of turmoil, and bring it back together as one nation again—all these different groups, within all this chaos, after so much anger from such a long period of time. In a brilliant interview, Oprah Winfrey asked him, "How does a man spend 27 years in prison by an oppressor and come out of that experience, not with a heart of stone, but a heart that is willing to forgive?" And he said, "First let me say that it is a great tragedy to spend the best part of your life in prison. But although it looks ironical, there are advantages in that. If I had not been in prison, I would not have been able to achieve the most difficult task in life—and that is, changing yourself. I would not have had that opportunity. I had that opportunity because in prison, you have what we do not have in our work outside of prison—the opportunity to sit down and think. To try to change yourself is a process."

In the world today, besides all the uncertainty—economically, politically, and in our lives—we're stressed, and we're busy. There's so much change happening that what we naturally try to do is to hold on and keep things the way they are. And it's only when we have time to be quiet and inside our thoughts, and this is key—to have the experiences to think about, that we really change. So how does this happen? Do we think about what we learned in a chart or graph and continue to remember an experience from that? We don't think so. Stories create experiences we may feel for a long time after we talked about them or heard them. When we are alone, when we have time to think, it's the experiences that we recall that may lead us to see the world and ourselves differently.

As we discuss a story with distributors and sometimes with customers, I think back to something Steve Denning said in an earlier chapter: storytelling is a dance; it isn't one person telling someone else, "you should change; this would be better if you would be this way." How much is the person going to be thinking about it a month later if it's just something that they're told, and they don't experience anything in that conversation? When you are telling a story—and more importantly, when you are inspiring a story from someone else—then the whole conversation, whether it's 2 people having the conversation or 20, the whole exchange becomes a dance. It goes back and forth and then back and forth again. And, most importantly, if you really listen and you really want to know, the sincerity, honesty, that comes out of the exchange of stories becomes an energizing experience. People walk away from something like that energized— they feel heard, even validated. They can feel it buzzing in them, in their gut, in their heart. With this energy they can possibly begin to see something new.

Going back to why we think that story of Mandela is so important: why does it make us think about the things that might lead to change, change that would be good for us and for other people? It's because we're thinking about it later, we're reminded of it, the experience doesn't—go away. Sometimes it just pops back into our mind, and we might analyze it and review it in our mind, but we feel it inside our gut and our heart because it moves us in some way that is unique to us and our lens. And because we keep thinking about it we talk to somebody else about it; that's how the story keeps going.

Learning to See the World in a New Way

So this book is about learning to see the world in a new way. Once you realize that the way you see the world is just the way you happen to be seeing it *right now*, only then are you aware of yourself, of your own lens. You realize that it also changes over time. When you finally see that, then you can really begin to listen to and care about what other people are saying. This is so against our nature—this letting go of control. It's a pretty scary thing in a lot of ways—to let go of the way you see the world. It can be scary to realize all the complexity and to recognize and accept other people's ideas and their perceptions. But although in one way it's scary, in another it's exciting, because suddenly you're so much freer; you're not working so hard to keep everything the way you perceive it.

And ultimately, by letting go of control, by being open to the other person's story as well as sharing your own, you are giving the power away. In the end, it is not about being in control. It's not about being the most powerful. It's about making everyone else more powerful. And there's no more effective way to do that in a way that grows and lasts, than with storytelling.

SIX

The Role of Narrative in Organizations

Confusion is the word we have invented for an order which is not understood.

—Henry Miller[1]

Stephen Denning: Some Thoughts in 2004

NARRATIVE IN ORGANIZATIONS: THE STORY SO FAR

We began the discussion in 2001 almost with an apology for talking about the topic of narrative and stories in organizations—a topic that Larry Prusak said that many people in mainstream management and organization circles might think of as odd.

The allusion to the presumed triviality and insignificance of narrative and storytelling for the serious task of understanding and managing organizations contrasts sharply with the scale of the narrative terrain through which we have actually traveled. We have seen that stories and narratives permeate every aspect of an organization's functioning. Whether it is the chief executive raising money or promoting confidence in the organization's future like Lou Gerstner at a giant corporation like IBM,[2] or Katalina Groh for a tiny film company,[3] or the people who repair the machines at Xerox,[4] or a change agent who fosters organizational transformation at the World Bank,[5] or the languages and dialects that spring up in communities of practice as described by John Seely Brown,[6] or all the multiple conversations at watercoolers and corridors and stairwells categorized by Larry Prusak,[7] stories constitute the lifeblood of an organization.

The conversation suggests that narrative and storytelling, far from being trivial and insignificant, constitute an obvious and central aspect of every functioning organization. Indeed, the presumption should be the other way: any discussion of organizations that does not place narrative and storytelling at the center is bound to be misleading and incomplete.

Recognizing the importance of storytelling, however, confronts most of us with a fresh challenge. Given the widespread presumption that storytelling is trivial and insignificant, we now have to unlearn what we all "know." As with other things we have to unlearn, the unlearning will make many of us feel as uncomfortable as we felt when we discovered that to go left on a bicycle we had to turn the handlebars to the right. It will feel strange. It will not be popular. And yet once it is recognized, it will seem so self-evident to us that we will wonder how anyone could ever have thought any other way.

To gird us for this challenge, I propose in this chapter to:

- Recapitulate the reasons why storytelling occupies such a central place in organizations today;
- Glance backward as to why the importance of storytelling for organizations was not recognized earlier;
- Glance sideways at the growing academic recognition of the importance of narrative and storytelling in various fields;
- Glance forward and contemplate where narrative and storytelling may be heading in future.

Why Narrative Pervades Organizations

In order to help us unlearn what we have been mis-taught about the triviality and insignificance of storytelling, let us remind ourselves of the characteristics of narrative and storytelling that account for their pervasiveness in organizations and elsewhere:

- *Stories have salience to the lives of people in organizations:* Wit, succinctness, and emotional power contribute to it (Chapter 2).

- *Stories help us make sense of organizations:* Stories and narratives reflect our efforts to understand the often baffling context of the modern organization as it goes through transformational change (Chapters 2 and 4).

- *Storytelling is quick and powerful:* Purposeful storytelling can reach large numbers of people, amazingly rapidly. People get the idea, but not slowly and painfully by the accumulation of evidence and meticulous elaboration of multiple dimensions. Stories have magically rapid trajectories through the social fabric of organizations. Storytelling communicates ideas holistically. As a result, listeners can get complicated ideas not laboriously, dimension by dimension, but all at once with a new gestalt, which is transferred with a snap (Chapters 1 and 4).

- *Storytelling is free:* Storytelling doesn't require expensive investments in hardware or software. It doesn't involve recruiting expensive experts. Storytelling is the ultimate low-cost, high-return technology (Chapter 4).

- *Storytelling skills are easily upgradable:* Everyone can become a better storyteller: Though we all tell stories all the time, we are often unaware of it. Once we realize what we are doing, we can all learn not only to become better storytellers but also to use storytelling to get business results. Experience shows that skills in storytelling can be quickly improved even with people with little apparent aptitude (Chapter 4).

- *Narratives communicate naturally:* Storytelling is our native language. To use it is refreshing and energizing. Abstract language by contrast is something that we learn at the age of 8 or later and becomes a kind of foreign language that we rarely feel as comfortable in as our native language, storytelling (Chapter 4).

- *Storytelling communicates collaboratively:* In abstract discussions, ideas come at us like missiles, invading our space and directing us to adopt a mental framework established by another being, and our options boil down to accepting or rejecting it, with all the baggage of yes-no winner-loser confrontations. Narrative by contrast comes at us collaboratively inviting us gently to follow the story arm-in-arm with the listener. It is more like a dance than a battle (Chapters 3, 4, and 5).

- *Storytelling communicates persuasively:* When the listener follows a story, there is the possibility of getting the listener to invent a parallel story in the listener's own environment. The story so co-created becomes the listener's own, and something the listener loves and is prepared to fight for. Storytelling can thus galvanize action (Chapter 4).

- *Stories can communicate holistically:* Stories can communicate deep holistic truths, whereas abstract language tends to slice off fragments of reality. Storytelling draws on our "vast deep of the imagination" to convey the connections that are missing in abstract thought. At the same time, we must be wary of the unreliable story and the unreliable narrator and subject all stories to analysis (Chapters 2 and 4).

- *Storytelling communicates context:* Before the advent of instant global communications, there was less need to be aware of the context in which knowledge arises. When communications were among people from the same village or district or city, one could often assume that the context was the same. With global communications, the assumption of similar context becomes obviously and frequently just plain wrong. Storytelling provides the context in which knowledge arises and hence becomes the normal vehicle for accurate knowledge transfer (Chapter 3).

- *Storytelling communicates intuitively:* We know more than we realize. The role of tacit knowledge has become a major pre-occupation because it is often the tacit knowledge that is most valuable. Yet if we do not know what we know, how can we communicate it? Storytelling provides an answer, since by telling a story with feeling, we are able to communicate more than we explicitly know. Our body takes over and does it for us, without consciousness. Thus, although we know more than we can tell, we can, through storytelling, tell more than we consciously know (Chapter 3).

- *Storytelling communicates entertainingly:* Abstract communications are dull and dry because they are not populated with people but with lifeless things. As living beings we are attracted to what is living and tend to be repelled by inert things such as concepts. Stories enliven and entertain (Chapter 5).

- *Storytelling communicates movingly so as to get action:* Storytelling doesn't just close the knowing-doing gap. It eliminates the gap by stimulating the listener to co-create the idea. In the process of co-creation, the listener starts the process of implementation in such a way that there is no gap (Chapter 4).

- *Storytelling flies under the corporate radar:* In listening to these stories, corporate management doesn't hear anything strange or disturbing or unusual. It typically doesn't think "she's telling me a story." It simply hears a talk that is clearer and fresher and more interesting than those they have heard for a very long time. So the discussion moves on to the substance not the tool. When done right, storytelling is invisible to the listener. By contrast, when you get into an abstract discussion about the values of an organization, for example, whether the organization is really committed to honesty and integrity and so on, you either receive glib assurances with a total unwillingness to take a hard look as to whether it's true, or you get bogged down in a massive metaphysical debate about morals, and the management often decides to scrap the whole effort and move on (Chapter 4).

- *Storytelling communicates feelingly:* For all the talk about emotional intelligence, explicit talk about feelings can be cloying. Storytelling enables discussion of emotions in culturally acceptable and elegant ways. Storytelling encapsulates values. Unlike abstract communications, which tend to be dry and unfeeling, storytelling captures the context and hence the feelings involved in situations (Chapters 2 and 4).

- *Storytelling communicates interactively:* Unlike abstract talk, storytelling is inherently interactive. The storyteller sparks the story that the listeners co-create in their own minds. Storytelling is inherently collaborative. Abstract arguments tend to be adversarial, with my idea fighting your idea. Storytelling sidesteps these dilemmas, by inviting an interactive process of collective dreaming (Chapters 2, 4, and 5).

- *Storytelling is memorable:* We remember what we hear in a story. We forget the abstractions we hear because they don't touch us. We remember what is in a story because our feelings are reached and because the listener becomes personally involved with the story. Whether it is cultural stories of Ireland, the Middle East, or Kosovo or the organizational stories of Tom Watson in IBM, stories have a remarkable staying power (Chapters 1, 2, and 5).

- *Storytelling spurs double-loop learning:* Certain types of storytelling can reach quickly into the deeper recesses of the psyche and change values and attitudes very rapidly. It can help us to unlearn what we need to unlearn (Chapter 3).

- *Storytelling is key to leadership:* It is easy to talk about leading without blame or judgment, about inspiring. The secret of the successful leader is often storytelling (Chapters 1 and 4).

- **Storytelling builds authenticity:** There has long been a concern that, born as original individuals, how is it that we die as copies? Today the concerns are sharper than ever. The molds that abstractions represent are a key ingredient in the phenomenon. Storytelling can rebuild authenticity by enabling the speaker articulate the speaker's unique viewpoint. Developing skills at storytelling enables individuals be trustworthy, real, original, unique. The genuine storyteller becomes authentic (Chapter 4).

- **Storytelling re-connects the speaker with the spoken:** Written language has brought tremendous benefits, but there is a downside. Writing separates the speaker from the spoken. The advantage of writing is portability. The disadvantage is that the author of the words often becomes uncertain, even a blur. Today we are inundated with anonymous words, and the anonymity of the source can become a concern. Oral storytelling reconnects the speaker with the spoken. Living voice is connected to living reception in a way that responds to some of our deepest desires to be connected (Chapter 4).

- **Storytelling re-connects the knower with the known:** As a child we learn some things through direct apprehension. As abstract concepts start being drummed into us, we acquire propositional knowledge from others, knowledge that we don't have first-hand experience of ourselves, but which we are told to take on faith from others. As an increasing proportion of our knowledge comes from others, which is often in direct conflict with our direct sensory apprehension (e.g., the earth revolves around the sun), we become disconnected with the bases of our knowledge of the world. Storytelling helps re-establish that connection by linking knowledge with the specific context in time and space in which it arose, enabling the listener to live the story (Chapter 3).

- ***Stories are a large part of the economy:*** Storytelling constitutes a large part of the world economy, perhaps as much as 20 percent of America's GNP, or the equivalent of U.S. $1.8 trillion. In anybody's terms, this is a non-trivial figure.[8]

A GLANCE BACKWARD:
THE ENEMIES OF STORYTELLING

If the benefits of storytelling are so impressive and widespread, then why are they not more widely recognized? One reason is that for the last couple of thousand years, storytelling has been under a cloud of disapproval. Understanding the source of the disapproval is a key to recovering the power and benefits of this incredibly powerful technology.

Plato: It is hard not to credit Plato with much of the disfavor in which storytelling has fallen, since a literal reading of his masterpiece, *The Republic*, shows that about half of it is devoted to arguing that storytellers (and poets) be censored or banned from the cerebral republic he was describing.[9] But as Plato himself was one of the master storytellers of all time, for example, in *Symposium*—the dinner party to end all dinner parties—he must have been aware of the power of storytelling. Plato's arguments in *The Republic* made sense in the context of ancient Athens, when the main emphasis was on storytelling and there was little hard-headed analysis. But the modern world has gone too far in the opposite direction, with an exclusive focus on analysis and a dismissal of narrative. There has been an unfortunate tendency for Plato's followers to adopt what can be construed as arguing in *The Republic*, rather than what he himself practiced in the *Symposium*.

Aristotle: Aristotle helped implement much of the intellectual agenda of *The Republic*, by placing a huge emphasis on the taxonomy and classification of what we know. He created a model for science that left storytelling in a peripheral role of illustrating abstract propositions. Abstract knowledge moved to center of the intellectual stage, where it has remained ever since.

Descartes: The separation of the self from the world meant the supposed abolition of feeling and emotions from rational discourse. Descartes laid the foundation for the concept of a mechanistic world free of mind and spirit. Scientists, feeding on their success through experiment, began to claim that their experimental method was the sole guide to discovering the truth. *Scientism* emerged—the view that only knowledge generated by science is genuine knowledge. The antagonism toward storytelling may have reached a peak in the 20th century with the determined effort to reduce all knowledge to analytic propositions, and ultimately physics or mathematics. In the process, we discovered the limits of analytic thinking. We learned of Godel's proof of the incompleteness of arithmetic and began to absorb the implications of the indeterminacy of quantum physics and complexity theory, but the scientific dialogue reflects the continuing itch for reductionist simplicity. In academia, abstract knowledge is still dominant and scientism is often the underlying assumption.

To escape from the intellectual blinders of scientism, we must unlearn some of the most fundamental "knowledge" that we have been taught:

- We have to unlearn what we have been taught about the unimportance of narrative and storytelling
- We have to unlearn the machine model of the universe in general and of the organization in particular.[10]

In the field of organizations, the specific kind of human mind to which mechanistic impersonal explanation appeals is what John Seely Brown called in Chapter 3 the mindset of the chief financial officer. It is the mindset of someone who is involved in the Promethean project of trying to control the environment—whether it is the organization or the universe—and so eliminate unpredictability.[11] Given that the human race has been engaged in this Promethean project for several hundred years, it is going to take some time before we all realize that although the project has led to immense benefits, it can only take us so far. It will take us some time to learn to "work with the world," as John Seely Brown put it in Chapter 1, instead of only trying to impose our own control on it.

A GLANCE SIDEWAYS:
GROWING RECOGNITION OF NARRATIVE

When did the rebirth of serious interest in narrative and storytelling occur? Vincent Hevern marks the revival of academic interest in narrative and storytelling the 1895 work by Learoyd, Taylor, and Clakins at Wellesley College on the association of longer narratives and the experience of synethesia (unusual and mixed preception of sights and sounds).[12]

In the first half of the century, Carl Jung, Mircea Eliade, Joseph Campbell, and Vladimir Propp popularized the idea of myth and folklore in society. The last few decades have seen an exponential growth in academic studies of narrative.

Jerome Bruner cites W.J.T. Mitchell's book, *On Narrative*,[13] published in 1981, as a landmark event. It contained a collection of articles by leading historians, psychoanalysts, philosophers, and literary critics, all of them preoccupied with the importance of narrative.[14]

Now in 2004, narrative thinking is everywhere. The idea that human beings are defined and constituted by their narratives has come to dominate vast regions of the humanities and human sciences—in psychology, anthropology, philosophy, sociology, political theory, literary studies, religious studies, and psychotherapy.[15]

Until very recently, these developments did not seem to have had much impact on mainstream management thinking which remained firmly ensconced in a managerialist philosophy, that is, the idea that better management methods will prove an effective solvent for a wide range of economic and social ills. The organization has been generally seen as a systematic, monovocal, hierarchical machine. If it didn't always work like a machine, the basic object of management was to try to change it and control it so that it did act like one, and in the process eliminate unpredictability.

More recently, the scene has been changing:

- A number of books have emerged to point out the important role of narrative, including Karl Weick's *Sensemaking in Organizations*,[16] Roger Schank and Gary Saul Morson's *Tell Me A Story*,[17] Annette Simmons' book, *The Story Factor*,[18] and Yannis Gabriel's *Organizational Storytelling*[19] (2000).
- The business press has also begun to highlight the importance of storytelling with articles in the *Harvard Business Review*,[20] Booz Allen's *strategy+business*[21] and the *Wall Street Journal*.[22]

The last decade has also seen the emergence of a post-modern strain of academic writing that views organizations as a pluralistic construction of multiple stories, storytellers, and story performance events, in which every story implies its opposite. At any one moment, one story may be dominant, but others in the background are clamoring for attention. For these theorists, there is no single, univocal reality—just a swirl of competing stories.

For instance, David Boje used a review of Nike and the anti-Nike activists to show the relationship between competing storytelling efforts. Nike tells stories about how well paid their employees are and how much better the working conditions are now than they were in the past. Meanwhile, activists talk about Nike's "dark side" and tell stories that question the legitimacy of its alleged practice of employing young female Asian workers to help accumulate billions in capital for the company. Customers also have narratives about Nike. Boje argues that we should not accept any one set of narratives alone as "reality," but rather embrace all viewpoints as part of the totality of Nike and trace the process by which Nike and its stakeholders evolve into something new. Boje sees Nike as replete with contradiction; between espoused and actual conduct; between public relations smokescreens and the workers' life spaces; between the chief executive officer's billions and the poor employees' meager wages. Nike is both itself and its opposite.[23]

While much of this post-modernist writing about the role of narrative claims to be value neutral, it has often adopted an inherently disapproving perspective of management. The assumption is that better management will *never* prove an effective solvent for our economic and social ills; inevitably, it will make things worse. In this optic, even "improved" methodologies such as total quality management are seen as thinly disguised maneuvers to get employees to work harder for less pay. This line of thinking will need to become more constructive in helping solve practical organizational problems if it is to have a significant influence in mainstream management thinking.

A GLANCE FORWARD: THE FUTURE OF ORGANIZATIONAL STORYTELLING

Where is storytelling heading? While no one can foretell the future, three broad trends are already in evidence.

Growing Recognition of Narrative in Management

Steadily increasing recognition of the importance of narrative in mainstream management is now inevitable. In the turbulent world of the early 21st century, narrative will emerge as a core competence of organizational leaders at whatever level. Universities and business schools will be drawn toward teaching narrative in courses.

Narrative thinking is contributing to an emerging view of organizations that more accurately reflects not only the traditional structural, process-oriented, control-based aspects of an organization but also the living, flowing aspects of organizations—where talking, thinking, dreaming, feeling human beings work and play and talk and laugh and cry with each other, in a way that is organic and self-adjusting and naturally innovative.

The Emergence of Narrative as a Set of Tools

Narrative is increasingly accepted as a powerful tool for understanding and leading organizations. Among the high-value uses to which storytelling will be put include:

- Communicating complex ideas and persuading people to change (Chapter 4);
- Getting people working together (Chapters 2, 3, and 4);
- Sharing knowledge (Chapters 2, 3, and 4);
- Taming the grapevine and dealing with rumors (Chapters 3 and 4);
- Communicating who you are (Chapters 2–5);
- Transmitting values (Chapters 1 and 2);
- Leading people into the future (Chapters 2 and 4);

A Richer Vision of Leadership

The role of storytelling in genuine leadership is also becoming more central. Thus, on one level, storytelling is a set of tools, but on another level it is something more than that. It's also a way for leaders—wherever they may sit—to embody the change they seek. Rather than merely advocating and counter-advocating abstract ideas of change, mere propositional arguments that lead to more arguments, leaders can enhance their credibility and authenticity through telling the stories that they are living. When they believe deeply in them, their stories resonate. This in turn elicits the authenticity of their listeners and generates creativity, interaction and transformation. When leaders take this right kind of risk, putting forward a vision without falling into the trap of trying to impose their control, then they radiate possibility for others and unleash their energy. Thus the meaning of the future for the people they lead is transformed and takes on the sheen of treasure.

CHAPTER ENDNOTES

[1] Henry Miller, *Tropic of Capricorn* (Grove Press, 1987, page 176).
[2] Chapter 1.

[3] Chapter 5.

[4] Chapter 3.

[5] Chapter 4.

[6] Chapter 3.

[7] Chapter 2.

[8] Chapter 1.

[9] Eric A. Havelock, *Preface to Plato* (Belknap Press, 1982).

[10] Richard Tarnas, *The Passion of the Western Mind*. (Ballantine Books, 1993), page 421.

[11] Chapter 3.

[12] Narrative psychology: bibliography and resources: http://web.lemoyne.edu/%7Ehevern/narpsych.html March 8, 2004.

[13] Chicago: University of Chicago Press, 1981.

[14] Jerome Bruner, *Making Stories: Law, Literature and Life* (New York: Farrar, Straus & Giroux, 2002). It contains an interesting short summary of the history of narrative in the 20th century at pp. 109–112.

[15] See Galen Strawson's review of Jerome Bruner's Making Stories, *The Guardian*, January 10, 2004. Strawson regrets the widespread acceptance of narrative.

[16] Karl E. Weick *Sensemaking in Organizations* (Thousand Oaks, CA: Sage Publications, 1995).

[17] Roger C. Schank, and Gary Saul Morson *Tell Me a Story: Narrative and Intelligence (Rethinking Theory)* (Northwestern University Press, 1995).

[18] Annette Simmons, *The Story Factor: Inspiration, Influence, and Persuasion Through the Art of Storytelling* (Perseus, 2000).

[19] Yannis Gabriel, *Storytelling in Organizations: Facts, Fictions and Fantasies*, Oxford University Press, 2000, Oxford.

[20] "Storytelling That Moves People A Conversation with Screenwriter Coach, Robert McKee." *Harvard Business Review*, June 2003, page 51; Stephen Denning, "Telling Tales" *Harvard Business Review*, May 2004.

[21] Bill Birchard, "Once upon a Time" in *strategy+business*, 2nd Quarter 2002. http://www.strategy-business.com/press/article/18637?pg = 0 March 8, 2004.

[22] (1) Julie Bennett, "Spin Straw into Gold with Good Storytelling." *Wall Street Journal*, July 30, 2003. http://www.startupjournal.com/ideas/services/20030730-bennett.html March 8, 2004. (2) Julie Bennett, "Storytelling & Diversity." *Wall Street Journal*. July 8, 2003. http://www.careerjournal.com/myc/diversity/20030708-bennett.html

[23] David Boje, *Narrative Methods for Organizational & Communication Research* (Thousand Oaks, CA: Sage Publications, 2001).

Further Reading

Aristotle: *Poetics*. Indianapolis: Hackett Publishing Company, 1987.

Aristotle: *The Art of Rhetoric*. London: Penguin Books, 1991.

Birchard, Bill: "Once upon a Time" in strategy+business, 2nd Quarter 2002. http://www.strategy-business.com/press/article/18637?pg=0 March 8, 2004.

Boje, David: *Narrative Methods for Organizational & Communication Research*. London: Sage, 2001.

Brook, Peter: *The Empty Space*, (London: McGibbon & Kee, 1968, reprinted by Simon & Schuster 1997).

Brown, John Seely, and Duguid, Paul: *The Social Life of Information*. Boston: Harvard Business School Press, 2000.

Bruner, Jerome: *Actual Worlds, Possible Worlds*. Boston: Harvard, 1986.

Bruner, Jerome: *Acts of Meaning*. Boston: Harvard, 1990.

Bruner, Jerome: *Making Stories*. New York: Farrar Straus & Giroux, 2002.

Campbell, Joseph: *The Hero with a Thousand Faces*. New York, Meridian Books, 1956.

Ciulla, Joanne B: *The Working Life: The Promise and Betrayal of Modern Work*, New York: Three Rivers Press, 2000.

Clark, Andy: *Being There: Putting Brain, Body, and World Together Again*. Cambridge, MA: MIT Press, 1998.

Cohen, Don, and Prusak, Laurence: *In Good Company*. Boston: Harvard Business School Press, 2001.

Cross, Rob, and Prusak, Larry: "The People Who Make Organizations Go or Stop", *Harvard Business Review*, June 2002.

Davenport, Thomas, and Prusak, Laurence: *Working Knowledge*. Boston: Harvard Business School Press, 1998.

Davenport, Tom, and Prusak, Laurence: *What's the Big Idea?* Boston: Harvard Business School Press, 2003.

Denning, Stephen: *The Springboard: How Storytelling Ignites Action in Knowledge-Era Organizations*. Boston: Butterworth Heinemann, 2000.

Denning, Stephen: *Squirrel Inc.: A Fable of Leadership Through Storytelling.* Boston: Jossey-Bass, 2004.

Denning, Stephen: "Telling Tales" *Harvard Business Review,* May 2004.

Eakin, Paul John: *How Our Lives Become Stories: Making Selves.* Ithaca: Cornell, 2001.

Gabriel, Yannis: *Storytelling in Organizations: Facts, Fictions, and Fantasies.* Oxford: Oxford, 2001.

Gardner, Howard: *Leading Minds: An Anatomy of Leadership.* New York: Basic Books, 1995.

Havelock, Eric A: *Preface to Plato,* Cambridge, MA: Belknap Press, 1982.

Hevern Vincent: *Narrative psychology: bibliography and resources:* http://web.lemoyne.edu/%7Ehevern/narpsych.html March 8, 2004.

Kahan, Seth: "Jumpstart Storytelling" http://www.sethkahan.com, November 9, 2003.

Klein, Gary: *Sources of Power: How People Make Decisions.* Cambridge, MA: MIT Press, 1999.

Latour, Bruno, Steve Woolgar, and Jonas Salk: *Laboratory Life.* Princeton, NJ: Princeton University Press, 1986.

Linde, Charlotte: *Life Stories: The Creation of Coherence.* Oxford: Oxford, 1993.

MacIntyre, Alasdair: *After Virtue.* Notre Dame: University of Notre Dame, 1981.

Mark, Margaret, and Pearson, Carol S: *The Hero and the Outlaw: Harnessing the Power of Archetypes to Create a Winning Brand.* New York: McGraw-Hill, 2002.

McAdams, Dan P: *The Stories We Live By.* New York: W. Morrow, 1993.

McCloskey, Donald (Deirdre), and Klamer Arjo: One Quarter of GDP is Persuasion (in Rhetoric and Economic Behavior). *The American Economic Review,* Vol. 85, No. 2, 1995.

McKee, Robert: *Story: Substance, Structure, Style and the Principles of Screenwriting.* New York: HarperCollins, 1997.

McKee, Robert: "Storytelling That Moves People: A Conversation with Screenwriter Coach, Robert McKee." *Harvard Business Review,* June 2003, p. 51.

Mitchell, W.J.T. ed.: *On Narrative*, Chicago: University of Chicago Press, 1981.

Nash, Cristopher: *Narrative in Culture: The Uses of Storytelling in the Sciences, Philosophy and Literature.* London: Routledge, 1990.

Neuhauser, Peg: *Corporate Legends and Lore: The Power of Storytelling as a Management Tool.* New York: McGraw-Hill, 1993.

Nisbett, Richard: *The Geography of Thought: How Asians and Westerners Think Differently. . . and Why.* New York: Free Press, 2003.

Orr, Julian: *Talking About Machines: An Ethnography of a Modern Job.* Ithaca: Cornell University Press, 1996.

Plato: *The Theaetetus of Plato*, trans. by M.J. Levett, Indianopolis: Hackett, 1990.

Polkinghorne, Donald E: *Narrative Knowing and the Human Sciences.* New York: SUNY, 1988.

Schank, Roger C. *Tell Me a Story: A New Look at Real and Artificial Memory*, New York: Scribner, 1990 (reprinted by Northwestern University).

Simmons, Annette: *The Story Factor.* Cambridge MA: Perseus, 2000.

Snowden, David: "Narrative Patterns: The perils and possibilities of using story in organisations" in Lesser, Eric, and Prusak, Larry, eds.: *Value-Added Knowledge: Insights from the IBM Institute for Knowledge-Based Organizations.* Oxford University Press, 2003.

Steiner, George: *Grammars of Creation.* New Haven, Yale University Press, 2001.

Tichy, Noel M: *The Leadership Engine: Building Leaders at Every Level.* NY: HarperBusiness, 1997.

Vincent, Laurence: *Legendary Brands: Unleashing the Power of Storytelling to Create a Winning Marketing Strategy.* Chicago: Dearborn Trade Publishing, 2002.

Weick, Karl E: *Sensemaking in Organizations.* Thousand Oaks: Sage Publications, 1995.

Wenger, Etienne, McDermott, Richard, and Snyder, William M: *Cultivating Communities of Practice.* Boston: Harvard Business School Press, 2002.

About the Authors

John Seely Brown

Until 2002, John Seely Brown was the chief scientist of Xerox Corporation and director of its Palo Alto Research Center (PARC). Since then he has pursued a variety of interests. He writes and speaks extensively. He serves on the board of directors of several public companies. He is a visiting scholar on digital media and digital culture at USC. He also advises high-tech startups. His personal interests are still related to finding ways to use digital infrastructure to create powerful learning environments and to foster innovation ecologies.

Stephen Denning

Stephen Denning was born and educated in Sydney, Australia. He studied law and psychology at Sydney University and worked as a lawyer in Sydney for several years. He then did a postgraduate degree in law at Oxford University in the U.K.

In 1969, he joined the World Bank, where he held various management positions, including Director of the Southern Africa Department from 1990 to 1994 and Director of the Africa Region from 1994 to 1996. From 1996 to 2000, he was the Program Director, Knowledge Management, at the World Bank, where he spearheaded the organizational knowledge-sharing program.

Since 2000, he has been working with organizations in the United States, Europe, Asia, and Australia on organizational storytelling and knowledge management.

His website, which has a collection of materials on organizational storytelling and knowledge management may be found at: www.stevedenning.com.

KATALINA GROH

Katalina Groh was raised in Chicago and studied finance and economics at Northwestern University before becoming a commodities trader at The Chicago Board of Trade. Soon after beginning to work on independent feature films and documentaries, she was hired to help launch New World Entertainment's educational division, New World Knowledge, where she co-wrote and produced award-winning films.

In 1997, she founded Groh Productions, Inc., which produces and internationally distributes its learning programs, documentaries, animated films, feature films, and live learning experiences. In 2000, she launched a new educational series, *Katalina Groh Presents Real People, Real Stories*™, specifically designed to focus on the power and practice of storytelling and its potential to teach, transform, and inspire. Her film series is now in more than 82 countries. To learn about audience reactions to storytelling and discover newly designed methods visit: www.grohproductions.com.

LARRY PRUSAK

Laurence Prusak is a researcher and consultant who has taught in several leading universities on the topic of knowledge management. He is also a Distinguished Scholar at Babson College. Prusak is a co-author of *What's the Big Idea? Creating and Capitalizing on the Best Management Thinking* (2003—with Thomas Davenport) and *In Good*

Company: How Social Capital Makes Organizations Work (2001—with Donald J. Cohen) and is the editor of *Knowledge in Organizations*. He has also been published in several journals including the *Sloan Management Review*, *Harvard Business Review*, and *California Management Review*.

Index